Praise for *Catch Your Big Break*

"Catch Your Big Break lays it all out simply, concisely and systematically. Read it."
Sam Carpenter, author of Work the System: The Simple Mechanics of Making More and Working Less

"If you aspire to live a life on your own terms, the ideas found in this book will help you do just that. If you'll apply the knowledge shared, the sky is limit for you! Read it, use it, and be better for it!"
Josh Hinds
speaker, entrepreneur, and author of It's your life, LIVE BIG!
www.JoshHinds.com

"Steve Monte is more than just a personal life coach… he's the Monday-morning jolt of caffeine that most of us need when it comes to making life change. 'Catch Your Big Break' is a brilliant work that challenges your thinking and shakes some paradigms when it comes to not only finding the job you want… but also loving it. 'Catch Your Big Break' should be on the top of your reading to-do list if you're looking for change!!"
Jon Talbert, Speaker… Humanitarian… Motivator

"Steve Monte firmly believes, as I do, that a flourishing and fulfilling career does not require you to sacrifice family, friends and health as so many have done. 'Catch Your Big Break' will encourage you to execute 7 specific steps, backed by thoughtful risk, so you can achieve a transformational and successful life. I highly recommend this book and encourage you to take the first step….risk the certainty of your current circumstances for the possibility of a remarkable and thriving future."
Dr. Jon Wallace, President of Azusa Pacific University

Catch Your Big Break

7 Steps To Get The Job You Want And Get Ahead In Your Career

Steve Monte

Catch Your Big Break : 7 Steps To Get The Job You Want And Get Ahead In Your Career

ISBN 978-1-105-59877-7

Printed in the United States of America

FIRST EDITION

First Printing 2012

To Bethany and Noah. Your presence in my life
is a daily reminder of how much God loves me.
I love you to the moon and back!

Catch Your Big Break: The 7 Steps

1. Write down your goals and repeat them privately

2. Take stock of your current situation

3. Do something BIG

4. Position yourself to win

5. Pick a channel to share your message and stick with it

6. Seize opportunities in times of change

7. Invest in yourself

Table of Contents

Waking Up Full of Awesome
by Melissa Wardy

There was a time when you were five years old
And you woke up full of awesome.
You knew you were awesome.
You loved yourself.
You were strong, smart and beautiful.
You just knew it.
Do you still have it?
The awesome.

1. Introduction

This book starts with a simple premise: You are awesome. You're smart, talented and hard-working. You know that because of these things, you have the ability to succeed in your career and do some exciting work as a professional before your time on this planet ends. There's a fairly predictable formula for becoming an accomplished professional in any field: you work long hours, you read a lot of books and professional articles in order to keep up on the latest developments in your field. You keep your nose to the grindstone until someone farther up the ladder notices you and gives you a chance to do something bigger and better. Once you catch that big break, the common thinking goes, you'll get a raise, you'll rub elbows with important people and you'll have opportunities that would have been denied to you otherwise. Life will be filled with daisies and roses once you pay the price to get there.

That's the problem, isn't it? If life doesn't get great until we pay the price, and if we have to wait for someone upstairs to notice our hard work and sacrifice, it leaves a lot to chance, doesn't it? What if nobody notices? What if we make a few mistakes along the way? (After all, nobody's perfect.) What if, while we're working hard and waiting to be noticed, the things we sacrifice are the things we value the most: our families, our health, and our desire to live life in a community of people who know and care about us? What if "paying our dues" at the office takes longer than we expected, and life continues to pass us by during the years and years that we've got our nose to the grindstone, waiting to catch our big break?

Some people choose the sacrifice, working the long hours and trying to get ahead. A few of those people do get ahead. Other people tell themselves that it's okay not to get ahead in business because there are more important things in life. They've decided that they're going to have a fulfilling social life, or family life, or life outside of work in some other way. They sacrifice being all that they can be on the job. They sacrifice a fulfilling and rewarding career. They sacrifice giving their best to the world through their professional efforts because they've bought into the lie that says, "You either work hard in business and get ahead, or you have a fulfilling life outside of work; you can't have both." It's a sucker's choice. I think if you buy into the lie that you can't find fulfillment at work and in your life outside of work, you are the sucker. I don't want that for you. I believe you can find a job that pays well, provides opportunities for growth and advancement, and gets you excited to go to work each day without sacrificing a fulfilling life outside of work. You don't have to work 70, 80, or 100 hours a week to keep moving forward in your career. You don't have to put your relationships with your spouse, your children, and your friends on the sidelines to reach another rung up the corporate ladder. And you most certainly don't have to forgo sleep or neglect your health to make it happen.

There are more and more people like me saying, "I can have my cake and eat it too. I can have a fulfilling, professional career and get 8 hours of sleep a night or close to it. I can reserve time and energy to nurture a wonderful, satisfying marriage. I can parent my children, not merely provide, and give them my presence rather than presents. I can be a part of a meaningful community outside of work, and I can still get ahead in business.

This is the book about how to do that. I ought to know how because I've lived on both sides of the sucker's choice. I've spent time working for very little money because I valued other things and I believed the lie that says, "If you want to make a difference during your time on this planet, you can't do that and make good money at the same time." I also spent some of my early years working hard (50 hours a week or more), then coming home to take care of my son, cook dinner, and pay bills with the few remaining hours of my days, just so that my wife could also work 50 or more hours at her job. I won't tell you that time of my life wasn't helpful in getting ahead. I'll just tell you that it wasn't necessary for me or my wife to work those long hours and argue about who would do the cooking and cleaning because neither one of us felt as if we had time to do it. I won't tell you I didn't get ahead in my career by doing that, but I will tell you that it wasn't the only option. There's another way. This way is not without risk. It isn't necessarily easy but it is straightforward and simple, and I've laid it out in this book.

This way will not always be comfortable, and this way will point you in a direction that may make you feel like you're living on the edge. There *will* be some risks. There was a great TV commercial awhile back in which an insurance company reminded us that the biggest risk is not taking one. Pause for a moment on that thought: The biggest risk is not taking one. The commercial reminds us that life isn't about avoiding risks; it's about choosing which risks to take and managing the results in a thoughtful way. That's what I want you to do. You're capable of making meaningful contributions to your company and even your whole professional field. If that's your goal, you will have to continue taking risks in the process. I want you to make a contribution. I want you to give greatly and dare greatly. I want you to experience the heights of success. That means taking thoughtful risks. It doesn't mean risking your health, your marriage, or your children's development. It doesn't mean stabbing people in the back or shelving your friends. Instead, it means taking the best you have to offer the world and letting it show, even if that opens the door for criticism. It means biting off more than you can chew sometimes, and it means that when opportunity rolls by, you jump on board even though you aren't guaranteed a smooth ride to your destination. Be prepared to take some of these thoughtful risks as you implement the steps laid out in this book. Your success depends on it.

This was a transformative lesson for me when I learned it from my college roommate, Greg Driscoll. At the ripe old age of 19, I was a pretty buttoned-up kind of guy who didn't take risks. I did the "right" things, the expected things. I got stuff done and I stayed busy. Graduate high school at the top of my class? Check. Get a job and buy my first car? Check. Become a boring, safe-living 19-year-old guy? Check. I wasn't doing anything flashy, or even particularly noticeable. I was kind of beige. I was just going about "getting it done" when along came Greg with his mantra of "why not?" Why not climb the tallest building on campus at midnight, and rappel down from the top? Why not stack up furniture a couple of layers high in order to create stadium seating for the not-so-big-screen TV in our living room? Why not grow facial hair, pierce your tongue, and woo women with original love songs and guitar playing? That was Greg. He taught me about the upside of taking risks, and I'm thankful for that. That lesson from my early adulthood carried forward. During my late twenties I took a look back and realized I had taken some more risks along the way and as a result my life was better. But I also realized something else as I looked back at the types of risks I was taking in my career. I realized I wasn't taking enough risks and I wasn't always taking the right kind of risks.

As you read on and consider that it may be risky to implement some of the seven steps to come, think about the risk of not taking these steps. Think about whether it's truly important to avoid risk in the end. This book will talk about when to take risks and which risks to take, and it will lay out a formula for getting ahead in your career without degrading your life outside of work or killing yourself in the process. As this book goes to press in early 2012, I know dozens of people who are out of work and struggling to find something meaningful and profitable to do with their time. They're learning a bit here and there to help them conduct a better job search or be a better professional, but the bit-by-bit approach isn't working very well. This book isn't the "baby-steps" approach to getting ahead in your career. This book is designed to be transformational. There are ways to get a job in weeks instead of months or even years, as is the case for many people right now. There are ways to get promoted now instead of waiting for someone to notice you.

Introduction

If you're sick of working at a breakneck pace to try to get ahead and you're ready to do something different, turn the page and start with step one.

2. Your Goals Suck

Your goals suck. This chapter shows you how to fix that. **The first step to career success is to write down your goals and repeat them privately.** Most people do this wrong, if they even do it at all. Scores of great books have been written about how to accomplish your goals, and the collective wisdom contained therein bears repeating. It also bears implementing. Before launching into the details of setting and achieving your goals, spend a minute thinking about this quotation, by an unknown author: "The genius of an idea is in its implementation."

All the greatest wisdom in this chapter is worthless if you don't use it. Stop right here and make a promise to yourself that you'll implement what you learn in this chapter before you move onto chapter three. Taking that sort of immediate action is a habit you need to develop if you're to be successful in your career.

People are generally divided into two types in terms of their working styles. The first type of person is right-brained. These are creative people; musicians, artists, and comedians tend to fall in this group. For these folks, the challenge is often staying focused. If you operate primarily in your right brain, I invite you to choose a goal and as you begin to take action, take that action in one consistent direction. Keep moving in the same direction toward that goal until you reach it. That's what it will take for you to be successful. What many people find as they try to implement this advice is that they're successful in picking an initial goal and working on it for a number of weeks or months. At some point, however, a right-brained thinker will be tempted by something new or seemingly more exciting. It's sometimes called "shiny object syndrome." You might recognize this tendency in yourself. You're working passionately toward a self-identified goal, but then your enthusiasm starts to wane just a bit, and before you know it. . . "Oooh, look at that shiny new thing!" Without a second thought, you're onto something different. If this is you, it is imperative that you resist this temptation! It may be helpful to pick small, short-term goals with concrete deadlines at first. This will allow you to develop the habit of following through on your goals until they have been 100% accomplished. Make sure one project is completely done before moving onto the next. If necessary, work as part of a team and select someone else to hold you accountable. By practicing this habit, you'll take a significant step forward in your work life and find success much quicker than you would have otherwise.

Other people are more left-brained types. These are the analytical people who tend to go into professions like law or accounting or computer programming and for these logical, analytical thinkers the challenge is not focus, but immediate implementation. They get caught up in analyzing their goals: "Is this the right goal? What happens if I can't reach my goal? Maybe I have to change my goal. What are the things that I need to do first before I start going after this particular goal? What will my family think about my goal? Is this goal worded correctly?" The issue isn't focus. It's action. It's getting out of analysis paralysis and doing something. That's why I love the Nike slogan "Just do it." They recently ran the ad above that illustrates this principle perfectly.

I love that phrase just above the Nike swoosh—that's the truth:

"This shoe works if you do." Your *plans* work if—and only if—you do. There are no quick fixes, and no further analysis of the situation, after a certain point, will yield better results.

For those of you who are born left-brained and analytical, your goal is never going to be perfect. You've got to get moving towards that goal and hit that goal. Then if you hit it, and it's not quite what you wanted, go back and set a more specific goal. Just get to work. Do something. Put on your Nike shoes if you want to, but realize that the shoes won't work unless you do. All of the wisdom in this chapter about goals is worthless if you don't implement it.

Do you promise? Do you promise yourself that you'll implement before moving on to chapter 3? Because I'm not kidding. Just do it now!

Now that you've made the promise to yourself (you have, haven't you?), you're committed to taking action. Think through the following facts from a survey conducted by www.ThinkTQ.com:

- Only about 50 percent of people create goals challenging enough to ignite their passion, to inspire them to take action and absolutely, unconditionally commit to hitting those goals. 50 percent is not a large number.
- About one in four, 25 percent of people, convert the goals and dreams they're passionate about into measurable milestones and objectives. This is the only way to consistently make dreams become real, and only one in four people do it!
- Less than 11 percent of people, one in nine people, write down all of their goals in specific, measurable detail including target dates.
- Less than 2 percent of people create a detailed map of daily, weekly, and long-term goals, and take actions towards those goals every day. Two percent of people!

What this suggests is that if you want to be in the top 2 percent of people in your profession, all you have to do is create a goal high enough to ignite your passion and inspire you. Commit absolutely and unconditionally to hitting that goal. Break the goal down into tangible milestones and objectives. Write down those goals and objectives with a declared target date for each one, and create a detailed road map of daily, weekly, and long-term goals. Then take action towards them on a regular basis. There's a direct correlation between earning power and the power to set and achieve realistic goals.

Let's take a few minutes to break this down a bit further.

1. **Set high goals.** Jim Collins and Jerry Porras in their book *Built To Last* talk about creating BHAGs—Big, Hairy, Audacious Goals. That's the way to get stuff done.

2. **Be S.M.A.R.T.** with your goals. There's discussion about this in the research referenced earlier from www.ThinkTQ.com, but let me sum it up by sharing from my personal experience. I spent a lot of money to get a Master's degree in Social Work from Indiana University. That's a Master's degree in creating positive social change. If you are a social human being—which we all are—and you want positive change in your professional career, take it from someone who has a Master's degree in creating that change; I invested a lot of money and two years of my life studying the process for creating positive change, and the most significant lesson that I learned is summed up by the acronym "S.M.A.R.T." We talked about it over and over again. It was Master's degree 101. I got it in my introductory course and in just about every course after that. S.M.A.R.T. stands for Specific, Measurable, Achievable, Relevant and Time-limited. Make your goals measurable and then measure your progress.

3. **Be accountable.** Identify someone who will hold you accountable and set specific times for them to do that. If you don't have someone who will help hold you accountable—some sort of peer pressure leading you towards accomplishing your goals— you're missing out on a great opportunity. My long-time friend Jesse Cross is an entrepreneur in Indianapolis, Indiana. At one point he and I both recognized that if we watched less TV it would free up time for really productive things. We realized that the kind of TV we were watching was killing brain cells more often than not. I bet him that I could go longer than he could without watching TV, so we decided we'd put some money on the line and we'd add money for every week neither of us watched any TV. The pot would grow and grow as the bet went on. I think that bet lasted eight or ten weeks until, by accident, one of us got sucked into a really interesting news piece and ended up staring at the TV for about 30 minutes. That was one way I've committed to a goal at high stakes and had someone hold me accountable.

4. **State your goals in positive terms** rather than negative ones. Many of you have done the exercise of not thinking about a purple elephant. It's really hard because the minute someone says, "Don't think about a purple elephant," a purple elephant is exactly what enters your mind. If you say, "I don't want to smoke. Don't smoke. Don't smoke," what your mind hears is "smoke, smoke, smoke" and it's very difficult to avoid smoking. But if you focus instead on breathing clean air and dealing with stress by drinking water or eating something healthy instead of smoking, and then you implement that, you may find yourself eating a bit more but you will find yourself thinking about smoking less and actually smoking less. So state your goals in

11

positive terms rather than negative ones. In this example, you're also replacing a habit that's destructive to your health with one that's constructive.

5. **Be true to yourself** and make goals about which you are both passionate and committed. If your parents want you to become a doctor or a lawyer and you don't want to, don't set either of those as a goal just to make your parents happy. I'm not speaking from personal experience on that one, but I know other people who have felt pressured into significant life decisions in order to keep a loved one happy. Set goals that you personally are passionate about. When you have identified a potential goal, make sure you are committed to seeing it through. Do some research. Talk to others when needed and identify the cost of accomplishing your goal. Consider whose opinion really matters to you, and discuss your potential goal only with those people. When you believe that you have enough accurate information about your goal, make a definite decision about whether you will pursue it. (Incidentally, I make decisions based on the formula taught by former secretary of state Colin Powell, which states that once you've acquired 40 to 70% of all the information that could be available about a decision, go with your gut. Doing so will keep you moving forward and prevent "analysis paralysis" from setting in.)

When I made the decision to write this book, for example, it was something that nobody close to me—not even my wife—actively encouraged me to do before I made the commitment to do it. The reason is that I didn't tell them about it until after I had done my research, made a decision, and committed 100% to making it happen. The goal came from deep inside myself for a variety of personal and professional reasons. I believe I have a valuable message to share with young professionals out in the world. I knew that I wouldn't get support from *all* of the important people in my life, but that was not a relevant factor when I set that goal and committed myself to accomplishing it. I wrote this book because I was passionate about the subject and I wanted to help its readers experience the kind of career success that I have experienced by applying the principles I've learned. Set goals only in areas where you are passionate and committed to achieving them.

6. **Know the benefits** that will come to you when you achieve your goal. If you're currently a mid-level manager and you want to become a senior manager, know the benefit of reaching that goal. Find out what the salary is. Find out how much time you'll be expected to put in. Find out if the position comes with its own administrative assistant. (If you want to shuffle less paperwork, kiss the fax machine goodbye, and never type up meeting minutes again, that's a significant benefit.) If you know that moving from mid-level manager to senior manager makes the difference, identify that fact; when you know all the benefits of achieving your goal, you can use them to focus and drive you towards that goal. If your goal is to make a certain dollar amount, no matter how you think you'll reach that goal, know what you're going to do with that dollar amount because money is just paper. Money isn't magic and it doesn't make you happy. Money can't buy health, but it can buy good doctors. Money can't buy sleep, but it can buy a nice bed that may help you sleep better. Money can't buy meaningful relationships, but it can buy shared experiences. It can buy items to help express your love to people with whom you already have meaningful re-

lationships, or people with whom you want to have meaningful relationships.

7. **Change in order to grow.** For any significant goal that you set, recognize that you're going to have to change some habits. You're going to have to change your thoughts. You're going to have to do things differently in order to achieve that goal and put yourself into a state where accomplishing that goal is effortless. If you always do what you've always done, you'll always get what you always got. Albert Einstein once said, "Insanity is doing the same thing over and over again and expecting different results." You have to change in order to grow and accomplish Big, Hairy, Audacious Goals.

8. **Commit yourself at high stakes** to the process of achieving your goals. Make a bet, like the one about TV watching that I mentioned earlier. Put money down on it. Spend money to buy education—classes, seminars, books, DVDs, etc.—that will give you the skills or knowledge you need to reach that goal. Request time off from work and block time off from your calendar to take action towards a specific goal. Do whatever it takes to identify specific investments you can make in the pursuit of your goal. If you take your time, your talent, and your worldly treasure and throw it all at your goal, your heart, body, and mind will follow after it.

After you've written down your goals on paper, it is important to review these goals on a regular basis and repeat them to yourself. Say them out loud when no one else is around. When you do this, you force your subconscious to grapple with the new reality you've created by setting these goals and committing to them. Your mind will go to work finding ways to accomplish your goals, and will seek out the resources it needs to move you forward. As you review your goals, feel free to expand on them or clarify them in any way that comes to mind. Your initial goal statements may be simple at first, and that's okay. Over time, as you consistently review and repeat your goals out loud, take a moment to write down any related objectives, strategies, and action steps that come to mind. These will be helpful as you move through the later steps.

Before you move on to the next chapter, take time to write down at least one Big, Hairy, Audacious Goal in as much specific detail as you can manage. Make it clear. Make it Specific, Measurable, Achievable, Relevant, and Time-limited. Then, identify at least one physical action that you can take today—right now—to accomplish that goal. For example, write:

I want to_____

As measured by _____

by the following date:_____

One action step I can take right now to accomplish that goal is

_____.

(For bonus points, go and actually do that one specific action that will move you towards accomplishing your goal before you turn the next page. Then write down a second action step. Go do it now.)

3. It Doesn't Matter Where You Are

Did you do what I asked you to do in Chapter 2? Did you write down your Big, Hairy, Audacious Goal? Did you identify an actionable step and did you take that step before moving on? If not, go back and do it now. Once you have done that, read on. When you have clearly identified your goals, written them down, and identified actions to get you there so that you know clearly where you want to go, then—and only then—figure out where you are now.

Until you've decided where you want to go it doesn't matter where you are. Too many times, especially in the counseling industry, well-meaning professionals advise us to take a look at our abilities and our current situation, consider our historical experiences, and only then discuss where we want to go in the future. I believe this is backwards. Too many people sell themselves short and set their sights too low because that's what their current and past experiences indicate are appropriate. I tell people that the "you" you were in the past and the "you" you are today are nothing compared to the "you" you can be in the future. First, decide where you want to go, then figure out where you are now and how to get where you're going. **This is the second step on the road to career success; take stock of your current situation.**

To accomplish this, do a self-assessment; honestly and soberly consider your skills and abilities, your strengths and weaknesses, and your personality and workplace behaviors in order to get where you want to go. Your spouse, a trusted coworker, or a longtime friend can be a big help with this. Until you understand where you are in relation to where you want to be, there's no way of knowing what specific actions to take to get there.

You practiced identifying actions in the last chapter. Perhaps some people can intuitively identify an initial action step toward goal attainment, but without doing some assessment most people aren't able to map out a clear and detailed route to their eventual destination. You have to have some knowledge about your personality and your personal strengths. Fortunately, some excellent personality inventories and strengths assessments are available and we'll discuss them in this chapter. Take a look at your performance evaluations from the last few years at your current job. I know that for some people this brings up a tremendous amount of anxiety and stress. Performance evaluations take some people back to high school where perhaps they weren't a great student and taking tests was not a positive experience.

It's okay to feel anxious about this step. It's not okay to skip it. You have to do it, with the recognition that you're an adult now. You're not in school anymore. In the tests that you're going to take as part of this step, there are no grades so you can't fail. The tests will simply give you feedback to help you fine-tune your strategy for getting where you want to go.

It's a cliché, I know, but it's true: If you don't know where you're going, you'll end up somewhere else. Perhaps my favorite saying along those lines is from Zen Buddhism, where it's said that if you're not careful to change direction, you'll end up where you're headed. The fact that you picked up this book and have read this far may be an indication that you're currently heading toward a place you don't want to go. You're looking for a destination that's even better than where you're currently headed. Perhaps you're frustrated with a lack of progress toward your destination, and doing some further assessment at this point is a valuable action to take.

Nationally-syndicated talk radio host and millionaire real estate investor J.T. Foxx says it this way: "I don't care how successful you are. Never stop learning—never stop educating yourself." I've had the privilege of meeting him, and I know he follows his own advice. The point applies here as well. You must continue to learn more about yourself—especially related to your strengths, your talents, and you deepest interests—so you can apply that understanding as you plan for your future success."

You have to take stock of where you are in order to get where you want to go. Until you know where and who you are, you're destined to live your default future instead of your invented future. We each have a notion of what our lives will look like if we change nothing. If we do just what we've always done, we'll get just what we always got. For many of this, us, this means a 40-, 60-, or 80-hour work week. It means a five-figure income. It means an occasional way-cool vacation followed by the credit card bill in next month's mail.

We don't stop and think about this default future and decide whether it's something we really want. We subconsciously act in ways that reinforce that future. But we have an alternative; we can live our invented future. You know—the one with the Mai-Tais, gently swaying palm trees, and white-sand beaches. The only way to get to your invented future is to clarify your goal, locate your current position, map out a route to your goal, and relentlessly measure your progress. This is the only way to success. (Thank you, Dave Logan and Steve Zaffron, for your book *The Three Laws of Performance*, which discusses the differences between these two futures). This step in the process requires taking stock of yourself and there are a number of questions you need to ask yourself. There are many great assessment tools available. Here are a few:

1. The StrengthsFinder assessment by Donald Clifton
2. The DISC workplace behavior profile
3. The Myers-Briggs personality type indicator
4. The Leadership Practice Inventory by James Kouzes and Barry Posner
5. The Multiple Intelligences Test, based on Howard Gardner's work

Visit my website, www.CatchYourBigBreak.com, for a complete list of personality inventories, workplace behavior profiles, and assessments of one kind or another, as well as instructions about where to find them and how much they cost. I have either personally used or evaluated all of them and I recommend them as potential ways to get ahead. Don't do all of them. Pick two or three and learn something new about yourself today.

Another task to complete during this step is to ask yourself the following questions:

1. How much money do I want to make?
2. What amount of money do I really need in order to secure my family's future, to give generously to other people, and have the kind of life that I want to have?
3. What is my ideal scene? (What time will I wake up in the morning when I'm living my invented future? What will I do before breakfast? What will I do between breakfast and lunch? Will I take a siesta in the afternoon once I'm done with my lunch? What else will I do in the afternoon? How many hours of work will I complete in an average working day? How many days a week will I work? What kind of people will I work with? Will I work at home or will I work in an office? What is my commute time to work? Do I have the option to work remotely? How many days a year do I travel? Do I like working on a computer? Do I like doing paperwork? Do I like working with people?)

These are all questions you need to ask yourself as part of your self-assessment.

In addition, Jim Collins in his book *Good to Great*, recommends asking these questions:

1. What can I be the best in the world at doing?
2. What drives my "economic engine"? This is to say, of all the things I do, what do people value most in my professional work? What do people pay for?
3. What am I deeply passionate about doing?

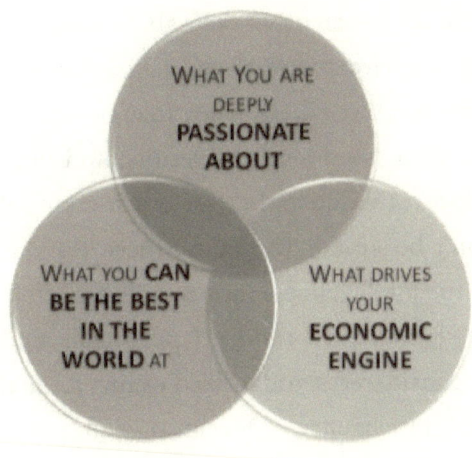

Where those three things intersect, make sure to note that. That's part of your assessment.

Then, think about your scores from the SAT, the ACT, the GRE, the MCAT or GMAT; they are assessments that you've already taken throughout your life; if you kept them, or you can remember the results, make sure to factor that into your overall assessment.

Ask yourself, "What do I know from standardized tests? Do I test well at all?" If you don't, that's OK. As I said before, you're an adult now; testing isn't about passing or failing. It's about what those results tell you. Perhaps you didn't score well on the GMAT. Perhaps you didn't score well on your medical exam. That doesn't mean you can't be a good medical professional. It may mean nothing more than that you don't test well.

Visit my website and look for the "Assessment" tab. Click there and you will find a downloadable worksheet containing all these questions. Take time to write down your answers, and capture them all in one place for future reference. This will be helpful for you as you create a roadmap showing how you can leverage your strengths—and find other people who can cover your weaknesses—as you move forward toward your goal.

You've taken many assessments of your personal style, your capacities, your strengths and a dozen other facts about who you are. Some people are afraid of taking standardized tests and hate even thinking about them because they aren't good test-takers. They may be afraid other people will think less of them when they hear the results, and they themselves may suffer from low self-esteem due to their poor test-taking abilities. If I've just described you, don't be afraid! In reality, these tests are simply a poor reflection of their true intelligence. Many people are intelligent in ways that aren't captured by standardized exams. I personally find it tragic that so many people have considered standardized exams to be the final authority on someone's true intelligence. Developmental psychologist Howard Gardner theorized in the 1980s that there were as many as seven different types of intelligence, and showed how standardized tests only consider a couple of those. He's added a few more intelligence types since his original theory was published, and he's an expert in this field!

If you're still worried about your standardized exam scores because you worry what people will think of you when they find out your scores, you may find it helpful to adopt a mantra that I've used throughout the years: "Those who mind don't matter and those who matter don't mind." When I was growing up, I often heard my dad offer his own, darker version of this idea. He'd say, "You wouldn't worry so much about what people think about you if you realized how seldom they think about you at all." Whatever you choose to tell yourself, remember this. The truth is there either way. It doesn't matter how you score as you assess yourself. What matters is that you know how you rate. It also matters that you use that knowledge to plan out the strategies that are most likely to lead you to success.

I highly recommend that as you're picking assessments, you pick some that allow other people to give you feedback. The Leadership Practices Inventory from Kouzes and Posner is one that includes feedback from your boss, co-workers, and subordinates. The Johari Window is another great choice.

Getting other people to tell you what they see in you is important because you can use that feedback; we're each our own harshest critics and we each have blind spots. Some of our own strengths and weaknesses escape our notice but other people see, and bringing them into your self-assessment affords you a well-rounded picture of who you are.

Information you gather from these assessments will provide fuel for the journey you have ahead of you. It will not benefit you to skip or skimp on this stuff. Make sure you follow the steps: complete two or three new assessments. Include feedback from other people in your own chain of command at work. Make sure you include your superiors. Include your boss' boss and senior management, if possible. Wherever the people know you well enough to give you the sort of feedback I've described here, include them and document the results in writing.

There's a more subtle magic in all of this that will help you as you move forward in your career. Taking this kind of inventory and dealing with the results in a mature way positions you as a learner. Every senior manager and executive I know understands that to be a high earner you have to be a high learner. Positioning yourself so that you're seen by influential others as a learner shows that you own your career and you aren't waiting for someone else to take charge of it. You want feedback, you know how to get it. You recognize, as life coach Kevin Eikenberry would say, that "feedback is the breakfast of champions."

360-degree evaluation can also open the door for conversations about your career and its development with your boss and co-workers. You've done your pre-work; share with your co-workers and bosses why you want this feedback. When I did this myself just a few years ago, I got a chance to say, "I'd like to run a place like this someday and I know I've got a lot to learn." It was an opportunity for me to say, in a subtle way, that I didn't think I'd had my last promotion. Naturally, you also want to be careful about who you share your goals with and when. There's no shortage of small-minded people around, waiting to step on other people's dreams because they don't have any of their own. I love the old saying "don't cast your pearls before swine" because it illustrates my thinking on the subject so well; don't share your most valuable wisdom and passion with those who won't appreciate it.

While I caution my coaching clients to carefully guard their dreams and goals, there is value in letting others know the general direction in which you're headed. Sharing your dreams allows others, if they wish, to hop aboard the bus and join you for the ride. At the very least, it clues them in to avoid steering you in a different direction. If you keep too tight-lipped about your plans, dreams, and your goals, others will make plans for you.

In the past, when I finally worked up the nerve to tell managers or bosses what I had in mind for my professional future, in some cases we parted ways. In other cases I got help in accomplishing those goals. In the best cases, sharing your goals allows people to support you at the times you need it most. A great rule to follow is this: Share your goals only after you've taken significant action toward them and you're prepared to accept whatever feedback comes your way.

When you share your goal, do it thoughtfully, strategically, and intentionally. Share it with someone with whom it's safe. Make sure this someone isn't going to trample on your dreams, but also be prepared for whatever feedback they give you. Don't share your goals with potentially influential people unless you're willing to listen to their feedback, and don't share your goals with people who have little potential influence unless you're willing to let their feedback roll right off your back.

Consider the story of British pop musician Howard Jones, who worked in a plastic-wrap factory at an earlier point in his life. He recounts that he told his coworkers during a tea break, "One day I'm going to leave this factory and go and do my music." Likely because they had no higher aspirations of their own, his coworkers ridiculed him: "No you won't, Howard! You'll retire from here like the rest of us!" While he may not be a household name, Howard Jones did, in fact, go on to have a 20-plus year career as a pop musician.

You must be fully committed and you must have taken some action before you share your goals with others, or you're in for a wild ride. Once you've done that, however, share honestly and use the resulting feedback to help you clarify and refine your vision. Listen carefully to the right people and you'll likely gain valuable information about how to accomplish your goals. After you complete the groundwork in this chapter, you'll be ready for perhaps the most significant step in the entire process.

4. Do Something BIG

I hope you picked up this book because you want to do something big with your life and work. People who just want to work a 9-to-5 job, go home to a warm meal, and watch an hour of reality television before dozing off to sleep don't really need books to learn how to do that. But "big" is a habit you have to cultivate when you want to earn big. **The third step to career success is to do something BIG.**

In chapter 3 we discussed the idea that to be a big earner, you have to be a big learner. Now I'll tell you that you have to do big in order to have big. Many of us know at least one person who is a millionaire, or a media personality, or someone who's considered an expert in his or her field. When we ask them about their success, we often find that they are in the habit of thinking big and doing big. To some it might have come naturally but others will have had to learn it. When I chart my own path to success, I look back at what I've done and I see a significant uptick in the level of success I've enjoyed during periods where I really grasped and practiced the habit of thinking and doing big. I first thought big, then I did big, and shortly thereafter I succeeded big.

I was someone happily employed but looking for my big break just a few years back. I assumed it would be a new job. I'd been looking for over a year. At one point I found myself reflecting on a book I had recently read called *The Go-Giver*, by Bob Burg. I liked how that title contrasted with the idea of being a go-getter. I decided I wanted to shoot for the stars. I wanted to do something big that would give back to my professional colleagues in a big way. I wasn't sure how, but I was thinking about it. Earlier, we discussed how important it is to change directions if we want to arrive at a different destination than the one toward which we're headed. Sometimes even a minor course correction can yield significantly different results. This was one of those instances.

One of my favorite coaches—one I've hired to coach me—is Raymond Aaron, an internationally-known coach with offices in Ontario, Canada. He once shared with me the example of driving a motor boat and zipping around a lake. As you zip around that lake, you realize that you're coming towards the shore on the other side. If you were to turn the wheel 180 degrees in the opposite direction, the boat would likely flip over and wreck; the course correction would be too drastic.

The idea of being a go-giver was for me a minor course correction. I considered myself a generous person at the time, but this lesson was significant; I realized that life and work are not about getting a bigger paycheck or a prestigious promotion. I had a strong passion for giving back in a big way and I knew if I gave bigger, I would also receive bigger. After reflecting on what I had read in *The Go-Giver*, I decided I was going to give back big to my professional colleagues. I wasn't sure how but I was going to get it done. When I shifted my focus there, my life shifted too. Within the next year, I got a promotion. I got a 25 percent raise. I formed my own coaching company, started seeing clients in the evenings, and made twice as much per hour as I was making at my regular job.

On a side note, something that book actually cemented in place for me was the idea that as long as I'm giving generously out of the right motivations, it's OK to receive, and in fact it's important to learn how to receive graciously. *The Go-Giver* talked about giving and receiving as breathing in and out. The highest-achieving athletes on our planet—who have developed huge lung capacity through habit-development and practice—take enormously deep breaths to supply their bodies with the oxygen they need to perform. They exhale during exertion, but they can't exhale forever. At some point they have to inhale. When they do it creates a need for them to breathe out again. So it is with us. If we give and give big, we also have to receive. Be okay with receiving.

Back to the point at hand. You have to learn how to give big if you want to receive big. Those are two sides of the same coin. So my question to you is this: "When will you do something big in order to receive big?"

How about becoming a leading expert in your field? Before you dismiss the idea, consider how one expert I know defined being an expert: "An expert is really just another professional who happens to live in a different zip code. We bring them in to speak at our events. Nobody knows them. We give them a good introduction and suddenly they're an expert in the eyes of our employees." Another expert I know talked about his expert status this way: "An expert is just someone who knows one percent more than you do. I happen to know more than you do on this subject. It may not be a lot more, but because you don't know what I know, you see me as an expert."

To put it simply, an expert is someone who knows how to do the following three things:

1. Position themselves as someone with specialized knowledge
2. Package their knowledge into attractive products and services
3. Promote those items in a way that gets them paid.

I learned that from motivational speaker Brendon Burchard, who runs an intensive, multi-day workshop on this subject. You can find out more at www.ExpertsAcademy.com. I don't get paid to promote his workshop, but if you check it out make sure to tell Brendon I said hello.

You can become an expert, and you'll learn how to accomplish big things in the process. Tony Robbins has taken the idea of doing big things and made it a cornerstone of his self-help system. He urges people to take what he calls "massive action" in order to create success. Awhile back, I lived in the same apartment complex with Wesley Goo, who had travelled and worked as a coach for the Tony Robbins Company for some years. He told me he went to work for Tony because he attributed a lot of the success he'd had to Tony's teachings. He became a student of Tony's at a point where he really wasn't happy with his life, and was able to make significant changes by using Tony's feedback around taking massive action. Knowing Wesley's story, it didn't surprise me when he went on to accomplish massive results, later branching out to start his own coaching company where he helps people completely reinvent themselves and create a more positive life in the process.

Another friend of mine, named Charlie Moore, decided as he was heading toward middle age that he wanted to be "Charlie 2.0" and for a number of weeks he talked about what it meant to be Charlie 2.0: He was going to drop some bad habits, pick up some good ones, and generally be a better version of himself. I loved the idea, and enjoyed seeing him successfully implement his plan. What would your life be like if you occasionally took time to upgrade your software, your thought patterns and personal habits, in route to becoming a better version of your true self?

Doing big is a habit you have to practice. What are some ways you can do this in your profession? Take a minute and brainstorm on paper what you can do as a professional that's big. This is a mindset you have to develop, so here's a little help: Big for you could be presenting your work at a conference or workshop. Write an article and get it published in a newspaper or professional journal. Create a video. Participate in training for your company and teach other people what you know.

One of my personal coaches, George Kao, says the human brain is designed as a creative instrument, not as a storage locker. It's time to take all those bits of information you have from your professional career, your life experience, and your education and start using it. Empty out your storage locker and start using your brain as a creative instrument. Do something so big that it scares you. Get out of your comfort zone. Get out of the rut that you're in. (My dad says, "A rut is just a grave with both ends knocked out.") Figure out what it is that you know well. If you're having trouble coming up with something, take a look at what the leading experts in your field are doing on a daily basis and do one of those things. And then do another one. Go on a radio show and talk about what you know, what you can do. (How do you do that? Remember the process for mapping out the steps we covered earlier?) Go on a television show. Write a book. Once you break these things down into steps, they don't seem as complicated, impenetrable, or intimidating as before.

Texas real estate millionaire Phill Grove also happens to do a lot of coaching around real estate investments. He says that at one point in his career he made a commitment to spend the first hour of his day exclusively thinking of big ideas and working on projects that could have a transformational impact on his business. He set aside all the activities that were just transactional: file this report, make a phone call to that person, respond to an email, talk to his secretary about the agenda for the day. He knew that he needed to carve out some space in his calendar, during the best and most productive part of his day, for transformational work. And he attributes a dramatic increase in his success at that particular point of his life to this single habit. Guy Kawasaki, the "evangelist" for the Apple brand, said it this way: "Create like a god. Command like a king. Work like a slave." Work doesn't have to be 40, 50, 60, or more hours a week. But you do have to work at implementing this idea. You need to set aside a significant amount of time where you work on transformational projects, projects that will have a significant impact. Set aside a few hours each week to do that sort of work.

Another picture of this comes from Mark Twain who said, "Eat a live frog first thing in the morning and nothing worse will happen to you the rest of the day." Brian Tracy, a well-known life coach, pulled this quote and made it into a whole book. He talked about the fact that we classify everything according to its urgency and/or importance. Most of us do lots of unimportant stuff every day. Urgent, sure: answering and making phone calls and emails, filling in forms and reports, stuff for which our boss or some important stakeholder in our company is clamoring. Then there's the non-urgent but important stuff like looking ahead, setting goals, getting training. The bit about eating a live frog first thing in the morning ties in with these non-urgent but incredibly important pieces. Those are the first things we need to do when we start work each day. first thing every morning. They're not enjoyable. They're frogs. But when you spend your best time doing these things, it will have a profound impact on your career. On the days I've been able to identify a frog and eat it first thing in the morning my day has been far more productive.

If you're looking not just for dramatic success but also for career satisfaction, this is a huge key. Eat a live frog first thing in the morning. Do the things that are both important and likely to get shuffled off because they're non-urgent. Do those things first. This is one way to take massive action. And take it in areas that you're likely to procrastinate. Get it done first thing in the morning. There are dozens more examples I could give you. Do what financially-successful business and professional people do. There's nothing special about this. These people aren't uniquely blessed by God. They're not lucky. They just do things that work and when you do the same, your life will immediately have the results that those people are having. In fact, it will surprise you how quickly your life will have the sorts of results that their lives have once you do the things they're doing. Back to what I said in the previous chapter: When you do what you've always done you'll get what you've always got. When you do what successful people have done, you'll get what successful people have got. It will happen.

5. Position Yourself to Win

In the last chapter, I briefly mentioned the importance of positioning one's self properly, and pointed out that this is one of the defining characteristics of an expert. The importance of developing this skill cannot be overstated. **In fact, the fourth step to career success is positioning yourself to win.** Consider the following story:

During morning rush hour on a cold Friday in January, a world-famous violin virtuoso dressed up in blue jeans and a t-shirt and stepped into a subway station in Washington, D.C. Over the next 43 minutes, he performed six classical pieces on a violin that was handcrafted in 1713 by Antonio Stradivari and valued at 3.5 million dollars. More than a thousand people passed by, many of them well-educated government bureaucrats on their way to work. How did they respond to this unexpected gift?

Three days before this subway show, Joshua Bell played to a sold-out theater in Boston and received a standing ovation. Guests paid a hundred dollars or more just to get a decent seat. In the D.C. subway station, however, he played for four minutes before someone even threw him a single dollar. Ninety-eight percent of the passersby didn't give him a dime, and even those who did rarely paused to listen. In the end, he collected just $32 and change.

It's a true story, captured in detail by a writer for the Washington Post, who set the whole thing up as a social experiment of sorts. What's the point? Even truly talented individuals, when stripped of the trappings that come along with success, fail to get the recognition they deserve. The same person can earn $40 an hour, or $10,000 per minute depending on the stage, the introduction, the attire, and the press coverage. (It isn't necessarily right, or fair, but it's true and it's a reality you have to confront.)

Positioning is incredibly important, and when climbing the career ladder one mistake that many people make is that they don't look for work while they're working. When they've got a job, they think, "Wonderful. I have a job and I'm just going to work my job." They don't look for anything else, and in doing so they leave themselves in a very poor position.

You can't do that when you want to succeed in your career. You're likely to find yourself unemployed, perhaps because of company politics or because the economy takes a downward turn. Regardless of the reason, it isn't until that moment that many people start looking for new work. They're forced into a position of begging for work, essentially, and having to explain over and over again why they aren't working currently. I recently heard of a middle manager who had hired a professional recruiter to help him fill a key position. He told the recruiter, "I don't want to interview anyone who's unemployed." His rationale was that all the best candidates would already be working for someone else, and he didn't want anyone but the best to come work for him. Though the recruiter tried to reason with him and point out that many great workers are unemployed for no fault of their own, the hiring manager was adamant. This thinking is not isolated to one manager out of a million. This is a common bias that we have to recognize, and we have to account for it when creating a winning strategy for our own personal careers.

If you're currently unemployed, I want you to take heart. Your situation isn't hopeless. You may feel a bit desperate to get back into paid employment, but the reality is that you have an alternative to begging. You may not see it this way, and you may be repeating the common mistake of positioning yourself as a beggar. We all know that beggars can't be choosers, so choose not to be a beggar! You don't have to position yourself that way.

Regardless of your employment status, recognize that you must begin the search for your next job right now. Even if you just started a great new job, it won't always be great. You must begin thinking about your next job now, and positioning yourself to transition smoothly into that next great job when it arrives. You have to realize that you can't wait a minute longer. The average length of time a U.S. worker stays in one job is 2.5 years. Start looking for something even better than what you currently have, and start looking now. The most successful people I know never stop looking for work.

In my own career, I'm currently working as a paid W-2 employee in addition to being a coach. I love the work I'm doing, and that's the only reason I am still doing it. I've committed myself to making a difference in the lives of disadvantaged youth, and my current role managing the mental health clinic for Santa Clara County Juvenile Hall allows me to do that. As much as I love it, I'm well aware of the fact that I won't be there forever. For me to accomplish my own larger goals, I'll have to move beyond that job at some point. I'm committed to providing valuable service to my employer for as long as I'm there, and I still make time to run my coaching business and test out other employment opportunities. This mentality affects me in a couple different ways, as it will affect you when you have adopted it.

First and foremost, from my first day on the job, I began implementing systems that would outlive me. I chose to focus on policies and procedures, and I also made efforts to develop people who would be there longer than I was. So when I leave, whenever that happens to be, Santa Clara County Juvenile Hall and the Mental Health Department (my official employer) will be in a better position than when I began. Others will carry on the work that I've started, and my goal is for them to have all the resources and information they need to do their work.

Second, I find myself often looking forward a few months, or even a few years, and thinking about what needs my profession will have at that time. I think about what trends will be shaping my industry. I think about what skills will be required in the workforce, and what I need to be doing in order to prepare for that. Then I get busy becoming the kind of worker who can thrive in the environment I envision. That's an important mindset. The knowledge that you won't be there forever needs to drive everything you do in your current position.

A friend of mine was the vice president of marketing for a large solar company in the San Francisco Bay Area. He knew what he was worth, what salary he could command in the competitive market, and he knew that he wasn't getting paid what he was worth. He wanted to move forward in his career, so he started talking to other solar companies about what work they had available and he found one particularly promising lead. He began talking to this company and found that they needed someone in their marketing department who could work at a very high level. As they were talking about whether he was the right guy for the job, and how he might be compensated, he walked into his current job one day to find out that the company would soon be filing for bankruptcy. He would soon lose his job, but he was able to transition smoothly into a job with the same title, working as vice president of marketing at another solar company. That would not have happened if he had taken the perspective that he was going to be with his old (now bankrupt) company forever.

One of the most constant and defining characteristics of life is that it has a way of surprising us. The way to deal with those surprises in a productive manner is to be prepared for situations like the one I described above. Successful people in the corporate world are always looking for their next position. The industry of corporate consulting provides a good model for this. Common wisdom in that industry is that people should always look for their next work assignment when they're in the middle of their current assignment. Their work cycle happens to be shorter than it is for the rest of us, as they change jobs every few months, and sometimes even after just a few weeks. If a consultant thinks a project will last six months, they're looking for the next project at least three months in, if not sooner. Before your career stalls—or you're unemployed—look for new work. Look inside and outside your company, look wherever you want, just keep looking. You've already done some of the hard work in crafting your vision, your ideal scene, and your goals for the future. Get moving forward and make them happen.

As you do this, feel free to spend some time researching the job market for your chosen profession. Take a look at www.salary.com or a similar website to find out how people are being compensated at a level or two above where you're currently working. Talk to other professionals in your network. Your professional network equals your net worth, so seek to expand it aggressively. Make it a practice to eat lunch with someone you don't know well and would like to know better, within your professional field, at least once a month. Seven out of ten jobs are won by someone who had a connection inside the company before they were interviewed, so make sure you're on the right side of that statistic.

Obviously many companies promote from inside. When they can't find the qualified applicant inside, they often place priority on seeing people the manager or the manager's closest coworkers know. People want to do business with people they know, like, and trust, so that's who they hire: people they already know. The statistic is that 70 percent of jobs are won by people who have a connection with the company already. For you, that means you have to make connections out in your professional network, with competitors, with other companies in your field, at different points along the supply chain, and with people in areas where you want to work or think you might want to work in the future. If you don't make those connections, you're going be part of the 30 percent. Your odds are only 30 percent that you will get the job if you don't know anybody inside when you're inter-viewed. Craigslist alone isn't going to land you the job you want.

One of my favorite coaches is Val Nelson, who specializes in teach-ing people how to network in non-traditional ways. She works with profes-sionals who are shy, or socially awkward, and don't handle the social scene very well. She teaches that there are a lot of different ways to network. Check out Val Nelson's website, www.ValNelson.com if you need a little help figuring out how to make your mark and make a living when you're not the most outgoing sort of person. If you're an introvert and you have trouble socializing, you will have to step out of your comfort zone in order to be successful. However, there are people who can help you, and you can learn to do it in a way that fits your own personal style.

Keep your résumé updated. If you need to, get professional feedback about how to use this important tool in order to market your skills and experience effectively. If you're trying to climb the corporate ladder, and you're trying to do that quickly, at some point, you will likely have to change companies. Of course, any time you change companies, people will want to see your resume. If you do not have a professionally-prepared résumé (and that doesn't mean you did it yourself in a way you feel is professional; it means a professional has given you feedback and helped you to create an effective marketing piece), then get it done. If you don't have a professionally-done résumé, you're leaving money on the table, and you're decreasing your odds of successfully moving to another company and up the corporate ladder.

Many coaching companies (including mine) offer résumé analysis and editing. This service identifies simple mistakes people have made that reflect poorly on them. It also identifies strengths within the résumé, and makes helpful suggestions about what items they can reorder. It points out what sentences they can rephrase, and how they can create a very professional frame of reference for people who want to know more about their professional work.

Also essential to positioning yourself effectively, whether you're currently working or unemployed, is learning how to prepare for and make a great impression in an interview. You must practice interviewing. As a special bonus to readers of this book, a list of ten commonly asked interview questions is available on my website, www.CatchYourBigBreak.com. Go get those questions now. The book will be here waiting for you when you get back.

Before you go into an interview, take the time to create written answers to these ten common questions, and practice saying those answers out loud. As you begin to practice, get feedback from a colleague, a coach, or a close friend about whether those answers reflect your own personal style and present you in the best light. As a hiring manager with years of experience interviewing people, one of the biggest mistakes I see people make is walking into an interview with no idea how to answer common questions. I say to them right up front, "Tell me a little bit about yourself." Personally, I choose to start interviews off with this question because I'm a busy manager and I don't always remember as much about the candidate as I wish I did, even though I've reviewed his or her résumé at some point in the recent past. However, I've found that I can multi-task well enough to listen to a candidate's answer while I glance at the résumé again. I find it's helpful to have them remind me who they are, and it allows me to recall interesting facts that I had forgotten. I can then put all the pieces together in my head and have a better context for the rest of the interview. The key point is that I want the candidate to tell me something relevant about his or her professional experience while I'm doing that.

People make the mistake of talking about their two cats, their spouse and the home they live in, and what they like to do in their free time. It's completely irrelevant to who they are as a professional. When a candidate goes on about their personal lives at the beginning of a professional interview, they're not just failing to put their best foot forward, they're shooting themselves in the foot. Their chances of getting the job drop rapidly as a result. Instead, script out exactly what you want an employer to know about who you are as a professional and what sets you apart from every other candidate that they're going to interview; few come right out with it, but every manager is asking, "Why should I hire you instead of someone else?" Script out the answer, memorize it, and when an employer asks you to tell them a little bit about yourself, give them your scripted answer. Don't tell them about your cat.

In addition to practicing your interview, it's essential to learn how to evaluate your own interview performance. This teaches you lessons that will help you in the next interview, and learning is important because there's always a next interview. Whether it's multiple rounds of interviews for one position, or an interview for your next job 2.5 years from now (remember that average?), you need to establish a routine of continuous quality improvement. How did that interview go? What did I do well and what can I do better? Write down those lessons. I have a tool that you can use to learn the lessons you need from an interview. I've developed it so that you can record for future reference the events of each interview. Think about whether you arrived early, on time, or late. Think about who you met during the interview. Think about relevant facts that you learned about the company, about the people you met, and about the position they're hiring for. Record exactly what questions they ask in the interview, or at least as much as you can remember. Do this as you evaluate yourself immediately after the interview while the results of that interview are still fresh in your mind. If you don't learn how to prepare for an interview, if you don't practice answering questions in a way that position yourself well, if you don't self-evaluate the interview in written form, you're passing up a huge opportunity to learn and grow as a professional.

The other point I'm compelled to make is that it's incredibly important to listen, when you're interviewing, for the interviewer's points of pain. Interview questions come in one of several different categories. Some of them are just informational; the interviewer wants to know a little bit about you. Some of them are about the minimal qualifications for the job; can you get over the hurdle of this basic requirement? What sort of previous experience have you had related to this work? Then there are questions related to some kind of pain the interviewer is in right now. This is where an interview can become an epic success! The pain may be something that the last person in the position couldn't do. It may be a new role or task that's been added to the position. It may be the very reason for creating a new position—to solve some sort of problem that currently exists within the organization. If you can identify the questions that are geared towards finding a candidate who can ease the company's pain, you can position yourself as that person and they will hire you because of the answers you give. Look for those questions. Better yet, come right out and ask, "What problems are you hoping the successful candidate will solve?"

The second most important thing you must do in an interview is answer any unspoken objections the employer may have about you. The interview process is a sales process; you're selling them on yourself. Talk to salespeople, if you have the chance, about how they answer objections their customers raise. The best of them will tell you they anticipate objections and know how to answer them. If you're 60 years old and you're applying for a job in middle management, you can anticipate one of the unconscious objections a hiring manager might have would be that you're too old. In this situation, you have to know how to answer that question, and how to reframe "old" as "experienced." Beyond that, you must be credible as you tell people how many years of work you have left in you so they can make an educated decision. If you have the energy, and you're someone who's going to work late into your sixties or seventies, find a way to work this into the interview even before your interviewer asks. Say, "Hey, I know I'm not the youngest guy on the planet, but let me tell you that people are living longer these days and I'm planning to be healthy and active until I'm 80. So I'm out here interviewing for jobs where I can do work I love, with people I enjoy, and there's no reason I can't continue doing that work well into my seventies. I may be sixty, but I can come over here and work for you for the next decade. The average worker, especially if you hire somebody who's much younger, is changing jobs every 2.5 years on average. You can have me four times longer. I'm not planning to jump ship or move up the ladder. I can tell you right now that I don't want that. I just want to spend the last decade of my career doing really good work." Isn't that a great answer to a likely objection the interviewer may have? You've positioned yourself as the right guy for the job, and now you've got a leg up on any competition from younger candidates. When you're on the other end of the age discussion and you may be seen as too young for the job, when you're a woman in a position traditionally held by a man, or a man in a position traditionally held by a woman, you must find some way that you're uniquely positioned to be an asset to the company and actively communicate that to employers.

The best time to do all this scripting and practice is while you're currently working, because the minute you're out of work, you're in the position of somebody who couldn't see the writing on the wall before their job ended. Employers like people who can predict things a bit further into the future and not end up unemployed. They're naturally suspicious of unemployed people. In the next chapter, we'll talk about how you can be unemployed and use that time well to position yourself as somebody who is still actively engaged in your profession whether you're getting a regular paycheck or not.

If you look for work while you're still employed, a natural question is, "What (if anything) do I tell my current employer when I'm looking for work?" That's a personal decision that will likely depend on your boss' personality and temperament. I think—unless your boss is truly an unreasonable person— there's incredible value in normalizing the transition for your boss, your co-workers, and yourself. Quote the statistics I mentioned earlier about the frequency with which people change jobs. Assure your boss that you want to do what's right for the company in addition to what's right for yourself. You're only moving out if you can't or won't move up. Hire a coach, if needed, to help you work through the details of how to handle this conversation with your boss, and strategize about where to go from there.

Years ago I was a manager at a small non-profit here in the San Francisco Bay Area and I decided it was time to leave the organization. I decided I needed to leave rather than working to move up the corporate ladder because, while I liked the work and enjoyed the culture, I felt that my opportunities for professional growth were constrained by the limited financial resources there. I knew there were better opportunities to learn and grow in other places, and I knew I could get paid better as well. So I told my boss. I told her particularly because the only other option was to talk about a potential promotion. My boss knew that I didn't want to be a front-line manager forever, and we both recognized that I had the ability to move up if I chose to do that. I didn't want her to rearrange the organizational chart or save a spot for me somewhere while I was planning to leave. She wasn't thrilled about it, but she understood it was the right move for me at the time. In the end she was able to support me, and gave a positive recommendation to my future boss when everything was done. She kept an appropriate amount of confidentiality around my decision so not everybody in the office knew, and because she was a safe person, it worked out better for me to share with her early on. It took me another three or four months, at least, to make the transition. We worked together in a professional manner, maintained a very good relationship and it allowed her some time to prepare herself and our team for the future. The decision to talk with your boss about a job search is not without consequence. If your boss is someone you don't necessarily trust and doesn't always have your best interest in mind, you should be cautious. Just don't let the question of whether to tell your boss keep you from looking for work.

Remember that networking is a critical component of your job search. It's not enough to look at online listings and expect to make a successful transition. It's important to know the basics of conducting a successful job search. Have your résumé professionally reviewed and edited. Learn how to prepare for an interview, how to interview well, and how to self-evaluate afterward. Focus on continuously improving the quality of these skills and you are destined to move forward in your career.

6. More Ways to Position Yourself and Win

So . . . what if you're unemployed? In that case, positioning yourself as a competent professional and, even better, an expert in your field, becomes critically important. After years as a hiring manager, some common tendencies have become crystal clear to me. When people don't have a clue how to go about getting a job, they do two things: First, they start looking through the help-wanted ads online, in the newspaper, and wherever else they can find them. Second, they start randomly sending résumés to people they know, and people they don't know. Many of us are willing accomplices in this. As a manager, I often get résumés from colleagues and friends who say, "I happen to know somebody who's looking for a job and I wanted you to have their résumé just in case you have something open." Ninety-nine times out of a hundred, I don't have anything open. What does this tell me? It tells me you don't understand what I need; you're wasting your time and mine. That's never a good way to start a relationship.

When I have a job open, you'll know about it if you're looking in the right places. If you use the tactics I just described, randomly sending résumés to people you don't know and desperately looking through the help-wanted ads, you're positioning yourself as someone who doesn't know what they're doing (regardless of whether you actually do know)! Do I want to hire someone like that? No, I don't.

You have to position yourself to win. Win with your references. This is one critical component of an effective job search that hasn't yet been mentioned. We talked about how to prepare for an interview, doing the interview, and self-evaluation in the last chapter. References are an equally critical component of an effective job search. On occasion, people I'm just beginning to coach will ask me if they should call their references since they've been interviewing for quite a few jobs. This always blows my mind! I can tell they've been giving a hiring manager the name and contact information for someone they worked with in a previous job, and they haven't even contacted that person themselves. This is a huge mistake! Your references should be people that you've intentionally selected and talked with ahead of time. They've given you permission to use their name and you know what they're going to say. This is completely acceptable; I coach people to tell their references what they want them to say. If you think you're a high-energy person, you're great with people, and you're a hard worker, it's OK to ask a reference, "Based on your experience working with me at our last job, can you honestly tell a prospective employer that I'm hardworking, high-energy, and I get along with people?" If they say no, don't use them as a reference. If they say yes, you're all set. Ask them next, "What phone number and email address should I give them?" This seems like a no-brainer, I know, but you'd be surprised how often this comes up.

I recommend that you have three references other than former bosses. Close professional colleagues are great people to use. Do not use family members or friends; they're biased when they comment on your work ethic and how effective you are as an employee. Unless you're looking for your first job ever, as a hiring manager I don't want to talk to your cousin, your next door neighbor, or a high school teacher. I want to talk with people who have worked alongside you on the job and can speak to your quality as an employee. Prep each of these people to say something different about you. If you've done your homework and you know who you are, you should be able to come up with three different unique strengths that separate you from other candidates. When a potential employer calls your references, each one of them should point out a different characteristic. So if you are hardworking, high-energy, and good with people, what a prospective employer should hear from your first reference is what a hard worker you are. They should be able to tell a story about an incident where you really worked hard and you went above and beyond the call of duty. Your second reference should leave "hardworking" alone and instead talk about how you're great with people; this person should describe in detail a situation in which you really engaged with a client or customer and made the company money/won over a tough skeptic/made a huge difference for the customer/whatever it may be, so that the hiring manager gets a well-rounded and positive picture of who you are as a candidate. It's part of positioning yourself to win. It's what winners do.

Imagine that you want a job in a technology company working as a salesperson. You need to find someone who works as a hiring manager in that type of company. If you don't know anyone who fits that description, talk with friends and family members. Or—why not?—walk into the building of such a company and ask who the hiring manager is. If you can get a few moments with that person, tell them you're interested in working in this field and are doing some research. Ask if you can buy them lunch and suggest your favorite restaurant. (This doesn't have to be expensive, but do consider a nice quiet place you can have a conversation, and stay away from fast food joints.) If they're resistant to the idea, offer to buy them coffee before or after work instead. Do whatever it takes, short of stalking or kidnapping, to get some time with them. Make it clear that you don't intend to try and talk them into hiring you. You are not, at this point, looking for a job from them. You want to take them to lunch and find out a little bit more about the industry and about the job they do. You can certainly tell them what kind of work you want and don't want. The important pieces of the conversation are asking them who's hiring and catching up on industry gossip. What kinds of candidates get hired? If somebody can pick up a skill, what would be the most important skill to pick up? What are the higher-paying skills? For example, in large metropolitan areas, it may be a particular language skill. Like many other managers here in California, I tend to hire Spanish speakers over candidates who only speak English. Language skills are very important, particularly in service industries and the non-profit world. In other industries, it may be a technology-related skill, or experience in a certain type of role. Get the story on very general industry trends and topics, and then also talk about more specific details, like whether any companies are hiring, who they're hiring at all levels, and so on. Sometimes companies are hiring for entry-level positions. Sometimes they're looking only for experienced workers. It's good to know what's happening currently.

If you do this kind of networking consistently and you do it for a long enough period of time, you will become the kind of person that managers want to hire, and the right job will come to you. When I sit down to lunch with someone who is doing this sort of process, I find myself thinking that this is an interesting person with whom I ought to keep in touch. Chances are I'll think about you when I do have a job if you're a good fit. But it's no use worrying about being a good fit. I'm going to contact you if you are. If you're not, don't try to shoe-horn yourself into the position or convince me that you have some sort of experience or qualification that you don't really have. There's a big difference between padding your résumé and actually developing yourself as a professional. If you're a software programmer, learning a new programming language may be a great way to make sure you have good job prospects. Trying to convince me that you know XHTML when in reality you've just started learning it is not.

So, when you sit down for lunch or coffee with a person who can help inform you about the industry, you can talk about yourself and who you are as a candidate, but you need to ask about the person you're meeting. Ask about his or her needs as a manager, and ask about the work they do as much as you try to talk about yourself. The most important message to send is that you're trying to figure out where you fit into the industry. You want to avoid giving the vibe that you're looking for any work that's available. As a manager, if I sense that you're just looking for any kind of job, I don't want you.

If you're selective and thoughtful about the sort of work that you're trying to get, say, "Hey, I'm really interested in this specific line of work. (Then describe the work.) What are the hiring trends with that line of work?" Now you're worth listening to. I value your question. Similarly, when we're trying to attract a romantic partner, most of us are smart enough to avoid giving the impression that we will flirt with anyone who has a pulse. Nobody's attracted to that. Someone who is selective when choosing a partner knows what sort of relationship they're trying to get into and is happy to ignore someone who doesn't fit their criteria. That person becomes attractive to a wide range of singles who are looking to go on a date.

Translate this scenario back to your career. If you want just any old job, you're not going to get anything. If you're very selective and you have a clear picture about what you want, you'll ignore opportunities that don't fit you and become much more attractive to all employers. That's the challenge of job-seeking while unemployed—presenting yourself as someone who's selective, even while you're thinking; "I really need to get a regular paycheck."

Some currently-unemployed people choose to consider internships or part-time work as a way to keep afloat financially while trying to land their ideal job. To them I say, don't just take any old internship or side job. These jobs may seem like they're easier to get into, especially when the pay is below the industry average. In reality, these jobs are equally difficult to get if you're positioning yourself poorly, and equally easy to get once you position yourself properly. I don't discourage people from pursuing internships or part-time work if that's what they want or need, but I encourage everyone to figure out what they truly want, and then position themselves well so they land a job the right way. In your case, these means that you have to learn about which companies are hiring, who in the company is doing the hiring, and who those people are hiring. You have to consider who your competition is, and identify your unique selling proposition. You must know what sets you apart from the crowd. This means you have to think for a change rather than blankly sending résumés out.

Your perfect job is at the intersection of those three circles I showed you back in chapter three. Do you remember them?

1. What can I be the best in the world at doing?
2. What drives my "economic engine"? (What do people pay for?)
3. What am I deeply passionate about doing?

If you haven't done so yet, go back and do the homework with the three circles and come up with some answers; identify clearly the intersection between all three. Figuring out what you do very well, what you enjoy doing, and what others are paying well to have done puts you in a position to win.

It's more than okay to go into an interview and say, "I want this job because it fits my strengths. I did my research and here's what we have in common. This is where I am as a candidate, and this is what I know about you as an employer, so this is where we are a good fit for each other." It's completely different from saying, "This is why you're a good company for me to work in." You give up your power in the relationship when you say, in what amounts to a star-struck manner, "Oh my goodness. This is such a great company. I would really love to work here. You guys have a good reputation in the community. I'm just so thankful that I got an interview with you guys." That isn't the way seasoned professionals and experts in their field speak. A seasoned professional or an expert speaks differently. They certainly give the prospective employer compliments but they're also careful to reserve for themselves some positive press. If I'm a very good job candidate and there's a very good company that I want to work for I'd say, "Look, I'm at a point in my career where I can be a bit selective about where I work. I know what's important to me, I know where I'm going to be able to do my best work, and I know my best work is worth what you're paying, because I've done my homework. I know a bit about your company,

I think I would really do well here, and I think you and the company would benefit from having me." That is a really strong value proposition.

I've been talking about experts and seasoned professionals, but even if you're young in your career, you can position yourself to win. You can position yourself as coachable. You can position yourself as a self-teacher, someone who is energetic. Someone who's further along in their career might have a harder time positioning themselves this way—it's one of the few advantages you might have over those candidates. Keep in mind that people who have 10, 20, or 30 years of work experience are often seen as less likely to listen or to give a boss credit for knowing more than they do. They're seen as less likely to keep up a high level of energy and enthusiasm. It's thought that maybe they're just putting in time and waiting for retirement. You have a lot of value as an energetic, young professional. It's all new and exciting to you. You're open-minded; you should definitely sell that and play it up as you're interviewing.

If you're young, leverage any kind of experience you have that's similar to the target position even if it isn't directly related. Imagine you're applying for a job as a computer programmer. If you can talk about experience you've had working with computers, doing web design, and writing code, and you can tie that all together to present yourself as someone who has a lot of technical knowledge. Talk about your knowledge of hardware in addition to software. That will bring you much closer. Discuss any previous successes you've had in any field, and talk about your work ethic. Talk about characteristics and behaviors you have adopted. Talk about your organizational skills. All of these things close the gap and allow a perspective employer to have faith that you can get the job done. Keep in mind that the greatest predictor of success in any job is success doing similar things in the past; beyond that, it's success in anything.

Everybody wants to hire winners. If I'm a football coach, I want to coach players who have won plenty of games in the past. If I can't get somebody who's a proven winner in football, I want to hire someone who has basic football skills but has been a winner in soccer, baseball, basketball or some other team sport.

Winners think just a little bit differently. I gave the example that a youth may be looked down upon in some circles, but that "liability" can be repositioned as the strengths of energy, coachability, and stamina where an older candidate might be seen as looking to mark time until retirement. Winners are able to present themselves to employers in a way that gets them hired. The world needs people who can do the thinking through those objections and then go into an interview and win the position. If your strength is being very analytical and thoughtful in your approach to your work, play that up. If you tend not to over-think things, if you just get in there and get the job done, play that up. If you have experience, talk about that. If you're young and inexperienced, talk about your youth and energy. You might be a natural leader or a natural follower. Feel free to talk about it because some bosses will be looking for the next leader to come up within their organization, and other bosses may be thinking, "I just want you to listen to what I have to say, and then go get it done. Just follow me and we'll get along great." Trying to guess what that person wants? There's really no win there. The way to win is to present who you are in the best possible light.

This reminds me of a conference I attended not too long ago. The speaker was a young Chicago real estate investor named J.T. Foxx. In addition to earning millions in real estate deals, J.T. also has his own radio talk show. He said he had earned, in the previous few years, several million dollars without really risking any of his own cash. As he was sharing some of the secrets that he'd used to do that, he said something about successful partnerships that you should think about. I wrote it down word for word because it was such a critical point. He said, "In order for a successful partnership to work, two or more parties have to bring something different to the table." He approached a number of partners who had money and said, "You guys give me your money to invest in real estate, I'll do all the work, and we'll split the profits 50/50." Then, he anticipated their objection: "Why, if we're putting all the money in, should we give you 50 percent of the profits? We need to get 80 percent." He told them, "Successful partnerships require the parties to bring something different to the table. In this case, you bring the money and I bring the work. While you're enjoying time with your family, I'm working. While you're relaxing, I'm working and while you're sleeping, I'm working even harder. You want to earn more and work less than you do right now, but that can't happen unless I do all the work. I know that you and I are going to do so many great deals together that one day you'll run out of money (to invest in all of them), but that doesn't matter because you and I are partners for life. There will be a time when you make money even when your cash or credit is not on the line. When it comes to partnership, my philosophy is simple: Loyalty, relationship, and results. I believe in 50/50 because I will be honest with you even when you're not looking." This was a script; clearly, he'd practiced and rehearsed this. The minute the objection to that 50/50 split came up—as he knew it would—he had the answer. People bought it to the tune of millions of dollars.

That's the sort of energy and work ethic you need to apply to job interviews if you want to be successful. You have to know exactly what you're going to say when an employer makes any statement that you identify as an unspoken objection to hiring you. Do your homework in advance to identify as many potential objections as possible. As you answer each objection in your own mind, write it down. Craft your response carefully so that it doesn't sound like a canned speech when you say it, then practice it in front of a mirror. Finally, practice it in a mock interview with a friend or family member until it rolls off your tongue as naturally as introducing yourself. That's the way to position yourself to win; Foxx had it figured out. He had thought about how to express the win for the other people involved in his endeavor, just like you need to think about expressing the potential employer's win in hiring you. That's how you win.

Part of adopting a winning mindset means spending time with other winners. Mike Warren is someone whose life inspires me in this regard. He had a difficult childhood; his story involves living in an abusive home, enduring his parents' divorce, and having to live with an alcoholic dad when he really wanted to be with his mother. He talks about making a conscious choice to take a road different from the one his parents traveled. He chose a different road, in fact, from the one he was then on. When I heard him speak, I was impressed by how all of these destructive experiences in his childhood gave him great authority to speak about dealing with toxic people in the workplace. He encouraged me to ask two questions about any person with whom I have a relationship. First, "What does this person have me thinking, feeling, saying, and doing?" Second, "Is that okay with me?" Because if it isn't okay, I have to make a decision to disassociate myself from that person. *That* is wisdom to live by.

Conversely, when you find somebody who has you thinking, feeling, saying, and doing positive things, you need to associate with them more frequently. You need to spend time learning from them and spend time sharing life with them. One thing you can do right now to implement this wisdom is to identify three people you know who are winners in life, and write down their names. These should be people who think, say, and do positive things. They're living the sort of lifestyle that you want. Contact each of those three people and propose a specific time and activity that you can do together. Spend time with winners and you will put yourself in a position to win. When you associate with winners, positive thinkers, and active doers, and you disassociate yourself from toxic people, you're that much closer to having your own success.

Thinking like a winner isn't always easy. If you knew what to do, you'd already be doing it. That's the value of hanging out with winners. That's the value of having a coach. Sometimes, just having a different perspective helps put you on a successful track—even better if it's someone who's got an inside view on something you need to know. They've had the kind of success that you're after.

At the end of this book is an invitation to "Forty-Five Minutes with a Professional Coach." Test-drive this process and if it doesn't work, walk off the lot without buying anything. The odds are you'll see the value and come back for more. I've worked with a number of coaches myself and I keep coming back for more coaching because it works. It helps me as a professional to further develop the winning mindset I need to build upon the successes I've had thus far.

The final thing I want to point out that when you're unemployed, you can get an internship or do volunteer work to implement these positioning concepts in a very practical way. For example, while you're looking for work, you could make a commitment to spend 10 hours a week doing something of value for a company you admire. Even if this work is unpaid at first, you'll have an opportunity to meet people inside the company and demonstrate that you can do the work. (Do you remember that's how most people get jobs?)

To implement this idea, make a list of 3-4 places that you consider ideal places to work. Talk to friends or family members who can introduce you to someone inside the company. If you don't know anyone who can do that, walk in the front door and make friends with the receptionist. Once you have your foot in the door, get an introduction to a manager and tell them something like this: "Hi, my name is Joe Smith and I'm really interested in the work you do here at XYZ Company. I understand that you're a manager in the widget production department, and I'm wondering if you have 20 minutes to talk with me about what you do. I'm sure you're a busy person, so we can find a time over the next few days that works with your schedule, and I'll buy you a cup of coffee for your time. I'll even deliver it to your desk if you'd like."(Hint: don't take no for an answer).

When you sit down with this person, ask them a few questions to make sure you understand exactly what this person and his/her department does. Then comment that this all sounds very interesting and you happen to have some free time on your hands, since you're not currently working. You expect this to be a pretty temporary situation, but you'd like to use your time wisely. Your goal is to gain some new experience, make industry connections, and add value to a local company in the process. Does the company have some work you could do, while you're in between jobs and working to figure out the best place to work next? The manager is likely to ask, "Are you looking for paying work, or volunteer work?" Well, of course you'd like to get paid, but that isn't the point in having the conversation. Your goal is to add value to the company in a place where they could use someone with skills like yours. You've got 5-10 hours per week you can commit to working, at least for the next couple of months. "What kind of skills do you have?" Answer this by promptly rattling off 2-3 hard skills that you do well. Avoid generic answers like "I enjoy working with people." Instead, state that you can type 60 words a minute, you're a whiz with spreadsheets, you love cold-calling prospects about new products, or you've got extensive experience with graphic design. Take whatever job this person offers, talk to whoever else in the company this person sends you off to meet, and thank everyone kindly for their time. Land a new gig and show up on time for your first day of work, whether it's paid or unpaid.

Investing your time in this manner positions you as a "go-giver" (remember that idea?), someone who is ready to work hard and learn from those who have more experience. If you end up unemployed longer than expected, you can repeat this multiple times, and take on small work projects with several companies in your chosen industry. The professional connections you make will be invaluable, and you'll be viewed as an insider when the right position comes open at any of the companies where you're spending time. Devote small amounts of your time to several different companies, rather than spending all your time in one place, so that you can multiply your chances of finding stable, paid employment in one of them.

This tactic cannot fail for someone with the confidence and solid work ethic required to test it out.

There's also great value in taking on interns or volunteers. This is another powerful positioning tool; if you can be the one who goes out and finds that young-and-hungry intern or volunteer and brings them into the company, you're bringing value into the company and you're positioning yourself now as a supervisor. You're positioning yourself as a trainer, an expert. You're now teaching somebody else how to do some of the work that you're currently doing. Before you think you could never do this or that you're not an expert/supervisor/trainer, remember the definition of "expert" in chapter 4.

My wife, who has worked in the field of nursing for many years, once shared with me how nurses learn new techniques or skills. They watch someone else perform the technique one time. Then, under supervision, they go do it. After they've seen it done once, they give it a shot. Then, they "teach" it back to the person who taught them. After that, they teach it for real to the next person, describing in detail what they're doing as they're doing it. They talk it out and act as if they know what they're doing—and by this time, they do. They call this process "see one, do one, teach one." I've adopted this phrase and use it in my own work because it reminds people that there's value in just jumping in and doing it yourself. It eliminates the objections—excuses, really—people have about trying things without "proper" experience. See one, do one, teach one. If you're hesitating about being a supervisor/trainer/expert, or taking on an intern or a volunteer, just jump in. Tell yourself, "I've seen people get trained before. I'm going to do some training and I'm going to teach people how to do this work. Why not me? Why not now?"

Chapter 7 will expand on this idea and give you specific ways to carry out the process of becoming an expert.

7. Pick It And Stick With It

When you're ready to take your career to the next level and position yourself as an expert, one of the most practical ways you can do it is to begin sharing your professional knowledge with others. **The fifth step to career success is to pick a channel to share your message, and stick with it.** There are many benefits to doing this, including the fact that it sharpens your thinking, it clarifies concepts that you know but are "hard to explain," (sometimes an idea crystallizes for you only when you have to teach it to someone else) and it puts the world on notice that you have something to contribute beyond what you do at your job. You may be thinking, "who will listen to what I have to say?" You don't have to have an answer immediately. Answering that question is part of the process. There are people that want—and need—to know what you know.

When my coaching practice was new, I listened in on a webinar done by a good friend who was already having success as a coach. He was sharing some of his marketing secrets about how people find him online. What he told me struck me as quite valuable and has stuck with me. He said that it's not just about getting found online, it's who is finding you and for what purpose? You'll get clear on that as you begin sharing and being productive. Production is more important than perfection. That's something you can take to the bank; repeat it before you go to bed at night and again when you wake up in the morning. I put production before perfection in anything. It applies to any of the principles in this book. The more you produce, the more you practice, the more adept you will become. This is particularly true if you're looking to other experts to see how they do what they do, and implementing the lessons that you've learned from them. Practice sharing your message. It will force you to think about where you're truly credible and knowledgeable, and where people will have an interest in listening to you or reading what you have to say.

I see a lot of people who blog, post YouTube clips, or use social media channels in an effort to share their message and establish themselves as experts. After a week or so, when they haven't experienced millions of hits, they declare the effort a failure. Then they try another channel, or worse, change their message and try again for a day or a week. If that doesn't work they move on again to a new channel or another new message. I'm here to tell you that is a colossal waste of time. It's not about finding the hot topic or the channel of the nanosecond.

Start by doing an honest assessment of who you are. Do you look good on camera? (This has to do with a lot more than your personal appearance. If you look uncomfortable on camera or you lack the technical ability to present yourself in a flattering light and produce a professional-looking video, build those skills if you're certain that video is the right medium for your message and your audience. Audio-only podcasting can be a great alternative if you don't present well on camera, or lack the skills or resources to produce professional-looking YouTube clips.) Also ask yourself the following questions:

1. Do I express myself best verbally or would I be better off writing Tweets, Facebook posts, or blogging?
2. What do I know that would make life better for everyone in my line of business?
3. In what area do I know 1 percent more than most of my industry colleagues?

It may take a little experimentation to find the answers, but once you've buttoned it down, stick with it. Pick it and stick with it. That's the title of this chapter and that's what you have to do. You will learn how to do it better and better over time. In order to establish yourself as an expert, you need to build your "brand" and part of good branding is being consistent. From Coca-Cola, we expect carbonated soft drinks. The corporation as a whole has its fingers in a lot of different kinds of beverages, but they use different brands to keep their stable of offerings from getting confusing and diluting the Coca-Cola brand. If Minute Maid orange juice was introduced under the Coca-Cola brand, or vice-versa, it would confuse the marketplace and dilute the Coca-Cola brand. The more you skip around and leave people wondering, "What will this person be trying next?" the harder it's going to be to gather an audience.

I learned the value of predictability and consistency years ago while doing a job search. I had done my homework and I decided I wanted a management position. At that time, I knew I'd meet the unspoken objection that I was relatively young. My predetermined answer to that objection was, "I may be young but I'm an energetic manager. I've had a great teacher/manager to provide me with a strong foundation, and I've got a few years of experience under my belt already." Young, energetic, well taught, and with some experience: That was my message to prospective employers. It didn't work. Time after time I tried, but trying to sell people on this line of thinking didn't work. I remember a specific interview when I was particularly disturbed by the outcome because I'd thought I was a shoo-in and I didn't get the job. The day after getting that discouraging news, a manager at a different company called me to say, "You're exactly what I'm looking for." Through it all, I was consistent with my message. I found someone who was looking for that young, energetic, well-taught manager with some experience. Had my message skipped from selling point to selling point as I went from interview to interview, what are the odds that I'd have picked that particular selling point for that particular manager? (Slim—I'm not that smart.) Had I tried to guess what each manager would "buy" and adjusted my story accordingly, I'd have fallen flat on my face. By consistently telling a plausible—and true—story, I was able to succeed and get the job.

Pick it and stick with it. Produce some material that really displays your professional expertise. Here are some channels to consider using: You may decide to make some videos, post them on YouTube, and send out some kind of announcement to people interested in your particular topic. If you do that, my general recommendation is, keep it relatively short. Do a lot of them if you feel like you've got a lot of information to share, and keep each video short so that people can get your info and give feedback quickly. If they like it, great! If they don't like it, they haven't had to commit half an hour to finding out. Analyze which clips were most viewed or received the most "likes" or "shares" and use that feedback to guide your choice of topics in the future.

Blogging can be effective, although it seems like everyone's blogging and very few people make it as professional bloggers. Most bloggers waste a lot of time writing stuff nobody reads. I don't want to discourage you, but I will tell you if you're going to do a blog, take it seriously; look at the experts in that particular field and closely observe what they're doing to gain an audience so you're not "writing letters to no one."

Another avenue might be to develop an email list. Before you begin, however, learn about the laws contained in the CAN-SPAM Act. One point in this law is that you have to provide a way for people to unsubscribe from your emails, even if you know every recipient personally. There are a number of good online tools for this: as of this writing, Mailchimp, Constant Contact, and several other front-runners are widely used by organizations large and small. Lastly, you may be in an industry that has a lot of conferences. If so, start applying to conferences and professional organizations to make presentations.

Regardless of which method you chose, it's important to keep in mind a lesson from the world of broadcasting. Experts in that field make a distinction between the signal, which is the valuable information, and background noise, which is the static you often hear between stations, especially on your AM radio dial. When you broadcast your knowledge, you have to send a signal strong enough to rise above the background noise. Choose a position on each significant issue, and state it clearly. Don't point out the merits of both sides of an argument. Don't discuss what other experts are saying without identifying your own opinion in the process. Your audience's time and attention are valuable commodities. Reward them with a clear, thoughtful message and they will continue to tune in. You must find your voice and then raise it above all the confusion and the uncertainty of the day. Quote what others say and then state clearly whether you agree or disagree. That's a great way, when you're first finding your voice, to get your professional knowledge out. Take a look at what experts are saying and then write the opinion piece on whether they have it right or wrong. Share how that point applies to current events. Lay out a concept and then talk about what you don't mean. Contrast it with the myths and misconceptions that are prevalent in your field. As you clarify your message and strengthen your signal, other people will tune in.

If there's something relevant in your professional field that you don't know, it's OK to say you don't know. Just don't turn around, then, and express an opinion about it—any audience worth having will walk away. No expert knows everything, but when it's important they research the facts and come back with an opinion. You might say, "This is coming up in the news, but it's so new I haven't finished reading through the research on it. I'll reserve comment on it until I get my head around the entire issue. I'm talking to a lot of people about this. In the next YouTube clip/podcast/blog post/email newsletter/Facebook post I'll have something for you because I know this is important." Your candor will resonate with your audience and they'll appreciate the next week's update even more because you've shown your professionalism.

When you've established your voice, you can then partner with people who have complementary voices to amplify what you're saying. Partnership is an advanced strategy for people who have moved into the expert arena. They have begun to develop their identity as an expert and they're ready to take that to the next level. Working with a coach, who can help you identify the places to look for a partnership and the ways to approach potential partners at that point, is essential.

To illustrate the potential of partnerships, consider an example from mortgage lending: If you're a mortgage lender, your business is very much in the news these days. Predatory lending, interest rates and default rates, and the general impact of lending on the economy have been discussed as much on Main Street as on Wall Street. Following the advice of this chapter, you would start by sending a strong signal, a message that cuts through all the background noise and helps people make sense out of a confusing topic. You might say something like "This is what to pay attention to regarding mortgage lending," or, "Here's how the average person on Main Street can expect credit-default swaps to impact their life over the next year." As your message begins to reach its target audience and they respond positively to what you're saying, you may be able to develop a partnership by reaching out to a successful real estate agent. You'd target real estate agents because they're helping folks buy homes and commercial property every day. In the process, they often become trusted advisors to their clients. They can amplify your message and extend its reach by getting it out to hundreds of their clients. They can recommend your work to people who are already interested in the subject. Rather than expanding your audience one member at a time, you're reaching out to the gatekeeper for a whole community, and having that person expand your audience by hundreds or even thousands at a time. This is the powerful leverage available from building partnerships. Going back to broadcasting analogies, partnerships are powerful amplifiers, whereas focusing too much on one-on-one networking can dampen your signal.

Whether you choose to share your message via YouTube clips, podcasts, e-mail blasts, or whatever, it's okay to start small with whatever message you feel is clear and strong—just get out there and start producing something. The mantra I repeat to myself is "production over perfection."

Silicon Valley venture capitalist Guy Kawasaki says it this way, adapting the words of the old Bobby McFerrin song: "Don't worry, be crappy." Don't worry about your first efforts being a little crappy. Just get going, get feedback, and implement that feedback to improve your product. Keep moving forward. Once you have a body of work and feel more confident with whatever medium you're using (notice I didn't say comfortable, because it won't always be comfortable) you can begin amplifying your message through partnerships and then repackage it for additional channels. When you have an audience that's consistently listening to a podcast, for example, they're more likely to read the e-newsletter you're launching. Layer something on instead of switching from one medium to another. Eventually you'll have your information going out in a whole array of channels and be able to build your brand across several media.

When I was in college, I heard a story about one of my classmates who ran into a homeless person digging in the trash. Being a compassionate person, my classmate wanted to help. He thought it was horrible that anyone had to dig food out of the trash just to get a meal and he wanted to help, but he didn't want to just help that one guy. He really wanted to make an impact on the issue of homelessness in the campus' community. There were a number of ways he could do that. He could start a non-profit organization to tackle hunger and homelessness. He could run some sort of awareness campaign. He could write the mayor and ask for funding for homeless issues. He just couldn't decide, so he went to a wonderful professor named Dr. Monica Ganas for some guidance. She told him, "Create anything but another excuse." I love that advice, I've implemented it in my own work, and I encourage you to do the same.

Before you turn the page and begin the next chapter, choose which channel you'll use to broadcast your message. For bonus points, draft out what that first message will be, roll tape, and produce something. Don't worry, be crappy. You'll improve as you go. If publishing makes you nervous, defer that worry. Just tell yourself, "All I'm doing is recording this podcast, or writing a blog in my word processor, and I never have to put it online. I never have to distribute it." Give yourself the freedom to create. This is a key component of having a successful career.

8. Never Let a Crisis Go To Waste

During the financial crisis of 2008, President Obama's White House Chief of Staff Rahm Emanuel famously commented, "Never let a crisis go to waste." He understood that the President could use the crisis to his advantage. He could accomplish significant items on his political agenda while everyone was clamoring for change. How we respond to crisis—and change—is critically important because it's in times of significant change that we find our greatest opportunities to succeed. **The sixth step to career success is to seize opportunities in times of change.**

Author Karen Kaiser Clark put it this way: "Life is change. Growth is optional. Choose wisely." In order to grow as a professional, you have to realize that in crisis, this reality is amplified. Furthermore, the person who can help others steer through a crisis will be a clear winner on the other side. Many of us grumble about change, big and small, or about events beyond our control that are perceived as undesirable or detrimental. Typically, leaders make change and followers grumble about it. If you want to be a leader in your industry, you can either make change yourself, or be the first one on the bandwagon when a change comes about, saying, "I'm willing to support this industry innovation, this new way of serving our customers. I'm willing to give it a shot." Every negative circumstance (perceived or genuine) has an opportunity coming right along with it. It's the yin and yang.

Raymond Aaron, one of my own coaches, lives in Canada where there's lots of snow. Of course people grumble about it. Raymond comments about snow, and life in general, this way: "See what others do not, even if it's right before their eyes. They envision only bad weather and traffic jams. You see delightful possibilities. Expand your vision. Widen your view. Enhance your scope. When you do, magical snowmen will mysteriously appear in your life, while others grumble about shoveling snow." I love that quote. Let other people grumble about the "bummers." Adopt a different perspective. Snowmen fall from heaven unassembled.

Here's how this works in your career: focus on what's new—a new technique for doing the work, a new product or service, a new location that's opening—and become an early adopter. Rather than being among those who complain about the change, jump on board and help out. This has made all the difference in my career and in my world. One time I was working for a small company, in a very stressful environment, on a team that had a lot of turnover. It was creating some morale difficulties, and I was young in the field. A coordinator, really a line supervisor, left her position and I volunteered to jump in. I knew it wasn't a particularly desirable position. This was the person who assigned each day's work to an already overworked staff. Nobody else wanted the job, so I jumped at it. To my puzzlement, people were grumbling about the fact that she was leaving and how sad it was that the position was going to be open. I said, "I'll take it." It got me experience, and it afforded me interaction—face time—with managers in the company. It wasn't much more than a year later that a new program was being envisioned. The more jaded and less ambitious people around me just ignored it. They seemed to be asking, in a very pessimistic way, "What the heck is our company doing?" All I did, initially, was give up one lunch hour to attend a brown-bag session about what this new program was. Six months after that, the new program was implemented. A new manager was going to be hired. I now had a year and half of experience as a coordinator. I got one of my first big breaks into management. Years into my management career, I now have a habit: whenever new innovations come along, my team will be the pilot team. We'll figure out what it is and how it will work out for the company. It positions me and my team well.

I offer you a word of caution, however: In the hunter-gatherer societies of our ancient past, the first person to eat the newly-discovered mushroom sometimes died. The first person to recognize the difference between that mushroom and this mushroom, to realize that the person who ate that one died, but the person who ate this one didn't, the first person to connect the dots correctly is the one we call the "early adopter." That person gets a tasty salad. There's a difference between being on the cutting edge and being an early adopter. Be an early adopter, rather than on the cutting edge. You don't want to eat the mushroom and die; you want the tasty salad. Don't invest too heavily at the front end, but place some small bets. I gave up one lunch hour in the example that I gave above. The bet was small but the payoff was large. I've invested an hour here and an hour there just to read an industry newsletter or research article to find out about a new trend. Many of those bets made no payoff, but one did. And one is all it takes. Place small bets and evaluate the results. Try to see losses early and cut them right away. Then, find those places where being the first to understand the meaning of a coming change positions you to take advantage of it and to win big. One skill that will help you in this effort is the ability to do what I call "pre-selling the benefit." Learn how to communicate to others in order to assess the potential return on any investment. What's the pay-off of this new initiative my company is taking? Ask others what they think. What is this change? Talk to the boss. How likely is this to happen? Is this something the company is already gearing up to do? Or are we kicking tires and doing research? What will be required to pull it off? What's the cost if we fail? Is this a high-risk, high-reward situation? Or is it low-risk, high-reward? (Maybe we're more likely to take advantage of that.) By having these conversations, you'll be able to determine who's invested in the change and who isn't, and also get a better sense of what the payoff will be for people who help implement it. Then, and only then, are you prepared to jump at those career opportunities that have the highest probability of success. You're a huge step closer to catching your big break.

Take a minute right now to write down some new trends in your industry, with a special focus on what your boss or top management in your company are talking about. Listen, when you go to that corporate retreat, or the all-staff meeting, or get the "from-the-desk-of-the-president" email, pick out the keywords. What are they talking about? What new ideas or new principles are they putting out there? What new industry trends are they discussing? Invest a little time to identify ways you can learn more. This is, again, a very important piece. Take advantage of change and crisis opportunities. Keep a positive mindset about them, because when they come along you have a huge opportunity to separate yourself from the crowd. While they're grumbling, you can be gearing up.

9. Price Check!

At this point, if you've taken time out to do some of the exercises suggested in this book, you're well on your way to greater success in your career. You're on your way to getting that job, getting that promotion, or getting ahead in your career some other way. You're several steps closer to catching your big break. Once you're clear about exactly what kind of big break you want, you must also grasp the concept that every opportunity has a price. I firmly believe the way we accomplish our dreams is that we first state clearly what we want from the world and then the world speaks back and tells us the price of that dream. After that, you simply pay the price and live the dream. This also suggests that you must, absolutely must, invest in yourself. You have to be the kind of person who has the personal and interpersonal capital to pay the price. Think of yourself as an organization. Your life isn't just about you. Imagine that you will eventually build an organization to fulfill the mission that is your life. **The final step to career success is to invest in yourself.** Invest the required time, money, or whatever else it takes, and you will accomplish your goals.

Michael Gerber, a famous writer on the subject of entrepreneurship, wrote that if your dream requires you to do it, you're dead. I attended a conference a while ago where he illustrated this point. In a room where all the speakers were millionaire entrepreneurs, Michael was the wow factor. For the better part of an hour he spun his tale of entrepreneurial success and detailed exactly how to get the right stuff done to accomplish that success. At one point he turned to me directly and, aware that I'm a coach, told me exactly what I needed to do in order to be successful. "Stop coaching," he said. "Create a coaching system. Make the system scalable and use it to transform the way other people do coaching. Create a coaching franchise prototype." I can't just do the work; if I want to be truly successful I have to think about how I'm doing the work. And I have to take the how and flesh it out in a way that I can hand it to other people. I must be able to see clearly how effective coaches work, do those effective coaching techniques, and teach everybody else to do that coaching the way I was successful in doing it. "See one, do one, teach one."

Toyota Motor Company promotes the idea of continuous quality improvement. As told in Jeffrey Liker's book *The Toyota Way*, the company says its job is threefold: to make cars, make better cars, and teach everyone else to make better cars. You have to invest in yourself and your own capacity in a way that allows you to do all of those things.

One of the people who has inspired me greatly in my career is Sam Carpenter, the owner of Centratel, the highest-quality answering service in the United States (according to him, of course, though I don't doubt it). His book *Work the System* describes how he transformed the small, struggling, poorly-run operation into an industry leader. Along the way, he learned that he had to quit busying himself with the day-to-day operation of his business. Instead, he had to step back and look at the work from "an outside and slightly elevated perspective." He noted that the successful leader's job is to "keep the wheels of the mechanism turning at full speed and with enormous efficiency." Note that his job was not to be the fastest spinning wheel. It was to create and then maintain a working system, constantly making improvements along the road to industry leadership. If you haven't read Work the System, I highly recommend that you do in order to help you adopt this mindset in greater detail. It's written by a man who lives what he's teaching.

Robert Kiyosaki, the author of the *Rich Dad, Poor Dad* book series, wrote, "The rich buy (or create) assets and systems. The poor buy or create liabilities." If you want to be successful, you have to create assets and systems that do your work for you.

Henry J. Kaiser was an industrialist in the early 1900s. You may be familiar with the Kaiser name. You may not know that Henry Kaiser made money as a ship builder, and then a producer of steel and aluminum. In each of those businesses, he focused on creating production processes that reliably turned out a product. Finally, he created the Kaiser Permanente health care system. He paid careful attention to business systems as he built his hospital and health care system. This probably is the most visible and well-known part of his legacy at this point. His system has done ground-breaking research on the impact of trauma and PTSD, and that's just one accomplishment I'm aware of due to my work in the counseling arena. They have countless other accomplishments and serve almost nine million healthcare plan members currently. You may not be Kaiser, but you must put effort into building capacity for yourself and your dream. Gather resources that will inform the work you're doing. Gather resources that you can share with others. Acquire the skills you'll need as you move up into management and executive leadership. Learn from people who have already accomplished the same goals you have. Find ways to automate things that you need to do regularly. Find ways to delegate things.

I heard someone talking not too long ago about working in a sales force. This person looked at the statistics showing how they moved people through their sales funnel, and they realized they were really good at pro-specting and qualifying leads. When they identified a person as a lead, they were really successful at building a relationship with that person and moving them a step further down the road so they officially asked for information about the product this person was selling. He realized at the same time that he was horrible at closing. He mumbled and fumbled and just did not present well. Then he realized somebody else on his team had the opposite problem. They were horrible about prospecting and couldn't focus long enough to develop and sustain a relationship with a potential customer. But somehow they could stumble through that process and get someone into a room to close the deal, and they closed it almost every time. Well, that was quite an opportunity. The pair simply arranged their work so the person who was telling the story did the prospecting and relationship-building.

When he had each potential customer to a place where they were asking for more information and expressing interest in the product, he sent in his closer. He spent his time on what he was good at: prospecting and identifying hundreds of leads. The other guy spent his time closing hundreds of sales. That's just one of the ways you can maximize the efficiency of your time and energy by paying conscious attention to how your system is working. You can make that investment in yourself and dramatically increase your results in the success you have as a professional.

One of my college professors pointed out another way to make that investment in yourself. She said, "Whenever you get the chance, go see 'the great ones.'" The great minds in each industry that we all talk about and speak of as experts are those people who speak at conferences and write books.

It wasn't too many years after I graduated that I took her advice and went to see a man named Salvador Minuchin. Maybe his isn't a household name, but to us in the counseling arena, he's one of the top 10 counselors of all time. He pioneered marriage and family counseling, particularly family counseling. He invented something called Structural Family Therapy back in the 1960s and 70s. He was 80 years old at the time I saw him. He told a great story about how often young college students would come up to him and ask, "Salvador, how are you such a great family therapist? I want to be a family therapist in my career. How do you do it so well?" He would tell them, "I think you have to have a family." That was his big advice. I didn't have a family at the time, and as I thought about what it would take to feel credible as a family counselor, I realized I didn't want to pursue it as a career goal. Learning that was well worth the price of admission. It allowed me to focus on my strengths in other areas.

Another way to invest in yourself, and your experience and knowledge as a professional, is to read. Leaders are readers. I don't know of a way to become an expert in your field, create something of value, and put yourself in a position to catch your big break that doesn't include reading voraciously. Drink from the fire hose. The best way to learn good stuff is to read good books. If you're reading a lot of books, the good stuff will rise to the top on its own. Anyone who tells you, "These are the only 2 books you have to read as a professional in your field," or, "This is the book," is probably trying to sell you theirs.

Popular career wisdom these days often suggests that you go out and find a mentor. Someone who will teach you everything they know and help you get ahead in your career. Someone who isn't your boss but has valuable experience that they're more than happy to share with you in great detail. I'm telling you that mentors are not a "miracle drug." The people you want as mentors are often busy people because they are accomplished people. Those who have valuable wisdom to share have to be selective about who gets to share their wisdom. I've often heard, and more recently experienced, that those who are successful at the highest level have no shortage of people wanting a piece of their time, their money, their wisdom, their resources, etc. Anyone you'd want as a mentor is unlikely to spend their time freely teaching you, because he or she is too busy doing the things you want them to teach you! If you're looking for expert guidance, you'd better look somewhere else.

The advantage to coaching is that it isn't a one-way street. You're not begging for someone's time and getting whatever scraps they throw you. You're in the power position by purchasing their time. You get as much as you want and can afford. Talk to a coach. Tell them what your budget is and find a way to get and pay for the valuable advice they have for you. By paying for good advice, you get quality and you get quantity. In my experience on both sides of the coaching table, nothing can replace this experience. Sure, get a mentor if you can find one who has the time for you. Learn from your boss too, but don't forget the coach. In each area of our lives that is important, we should get a coach, whether it's our relationships, our work, or a sport we want to play.

Many people say they can't afford it and I challenge them to rethink that notion. Perhaps the best way to illustrate this is by telling about my consultant friend Karen who spends time advising large healthcare organizations on major change initiatives they're planning. When she meets resistance to the changes that are being discussed, she reminds them to consider the cost of *not* changing.

It will probably help to think of this as opportunity cost: You can choose to buy 10 books for the price of an hour coaching session, or you can buy concert tickets. If, in that one hour, a coach's contribution can help you find the job you want, even one week sooner, what is the cost? If you're unemployed and a coach helps you find a job paying $40 an hour a week quicker than you would have without the coach, that's $1600 in your pocket minus maybe $150 for the coach's services. You're ahead $1450 on that proposition.

What did those books actually cost you? What about those concert tickets? They cost you $1700. Not only are you out the money, but you didn't get the job as soon as you could have. You didn't get the coaching, and the opportunity you passed up cost you $1600 in addition to the $100 that you wasted on something unproductive. You bought a depreciating asset that sooner or later will be worth nothing. The same opportunity cost applies to getting a raise, getting a promotion, or any sort of choice work assignment that a coach can help you figure out how to get. A coach can offer you perspective and strategy, pointing you in the right direction when you're unsure which way to go.

These results are not guaranteed, obviously, but you definitely won't get them if you refuse even to test out the coaching process. The best coaches are confident enough in themselves that they will guarantee your satisfaction. If you don't like your experience and find it valuable, you'll get your money back. Run, don't walk, from any coach who doesn't give you some sort of satisfaction guarantee. In my practice, I tell clients that if they aren't satisfied at the end of any session, they just let me know and arrange to pay a reduced price or nothing at all. In other words, you tell me what you think it was worth and if I only get paid $10 then I need to work on improving, so I can bring my A game the next time we have a coaching session. I can't guarantee results because you are responsible for implementing what you learned. However, I can guarantee that paying for good advice and helpful direction in your career is worth every dime you'll pay for it.

Author and teacher John Smart said it this way: "A part of our future appears to be evolutionary and unpredictable and another part looks developmental and predictable. Our challenge is to invent the first and discover the second." You can invent your future by using other professionals, people who can provide you insight into how you get where you want to go. They guide the way. They can help you discover which parts of your invented future can be accomplished through a step-by-step approach, and which parts of your invented future will require a bit of chance. It's in these places that you'll learn even more. You'll learn how to catch your big break by inventing it. That is a powerful thing.

10. The Next Physical Action

You've now seen the entire process and you can use it to accomplish your career goals, get hired, get promoted, and make good money doing work you love. What's left now is to implement this process relentlessly. You must take action or all of this is for nothing. David Allen, the productivity guru and author of *Getting Things Done*, says it this way: "We're all accountable to define what, if anything, we're committed to make happen as we engage with ourselves and others. And at some point for any outcome that we have an internal commitment to complete, we must make a decision about the next physical action required." I've pointed out a number of potential actions you can take in order to accomplish your goals. My website has more. Don't close this book before deciding what you want and what action you will take. If you implement this process, I know you'll move forward and experience many successes, big and small, in your career.

Not long ago, as I was doing the initial preparation for writing this book, I dropped my cell phone and cracked the screen, prompting a trip to my local Verizon store. I figured I'd use the opportunity to upgrade, but I hadn't given much thought to what kind of phone I wanted. As I hemmed and I hawed, I got very little help from the guy at the counter. It was as if he just wanted me to make up my mind and get out of his face. I didn't want to spend a ton of money, and I ended up taking something home that didn't really suit my needs, because it was a good deal. I went back a couple of weeks later to exchange it for something different. It was then and there that I met Jason Toledo. Jason was more than just another guy behind the counter. A working business-school student, he told me of the ambitious plans he had for his future. He helped me choose a Blackberry Bold, priced higher than I intended to go, and then he persuaded me to buy a protective cover so that I wouldn't damage my precious investment. The other guy didn't help me make any decision and he let me walk out of the store with a sub-par product. I don't remember that guy's name, but it'll be awhile before I forget Jason Toledo's. He had a structure for engaging me, and at the end of the day he got the job done.

Do you want to be successful too? Get something done. Identify the very next physical action you need to take to be successful. Whether it's writing some of your ideas down, calling someone who'd make a good partner, or recording a podcast that helps you establish yourself as an expert, make sure you get something done. As one of my favorite coaches, Brendan Burchard, once said, "Your life changes when you say, 'I'm hungry for something new. I desire something bigger and better for myself.' And you say, 'You know what? It's on me. I've got to own the situation.' Once you realize that the situation is yours, and you must do something with it, the only thing that remains for successful people is to go out and get it done." Will you do that? If you will, the world awaits.

Special Bonus # 1: Steve's Complete List of Self-Assessment Tools

Receive all of Steve's top-rated assessment tools to help you know yourself better and present a clear, consistent picture to your future boss before you interview. The list includes a number of valuable resources, including two 360-degree evaluation tools that will allow your bosses, co-workers, and subordinates to give you feedback about their experience working with you. An overwhelming number of personality inventories and self-assessments are now available via the Internet. Steve has sorted through mountains of resources and gives you his complete list of all the best tools that he's familiar with or has used himself. Visit www.CatchYourBigBreak.com and get the tools you need to become a champion!

Special Bonus # 2: Ten Common Interview Questions

Download this worksheet, which walks you step-by-step through some of the most common interview questions in use today. Learn the secrets of interview preparation that even many high-powered executives don't know. In this bonus, Steve guides you through the process of crafting answers that will have managers tripping over themselves to hire you. What are you waiting for? Visit www.CatchYourBigBreak.com now.

Special Bonus # 3: Discount On Group and Individual Coaching Packages

Read carefully because this is perhaps the most valuable secret in this entire book. This special bonus is available to anyone reading this section, even if you didn't buy this book. You've earned handsome rewards for taking the time to read through this small paragraph. Find a coupon worth $50 off any coaching package you purchase from Steve. Visit www.CatchYourBigBreak.com.

Special Bonus # 4: Forty-Five Minutes with a Professional Coach

If $50 off coaching services isn't quite enough to convince you to give coaching services a try, test-drive coaching with one of Steve Monte Coaching's top-notch people for 45 minutes of consultation—free of charge—and see the benefit you'll derive from professional coaching. You know where to go.

Acknowledgments

As much as I found joy in the creative process that led to this book being written and published, it would not have been possible without a great team of people behind me. My deepest appreciation goes out first to my own personal coaches. To Raymond Aaron for inspiring me to write, and giving me countless suggestions that allowed me to overcome all obstacles and get it done. To George Kao for his constant encouragement, and his reminders about the importance of growing my coaching practice in a sustainable way. And to Clay Collins for keeping it real, telling the truth, and teaching me almost everything I know about the interactive sales process.

Next, my thanks go out to Ken Hughes, Judi Monte, Paul Southall, and the good people at Lulu Enterprises. Your technical skills in editing, design, and marketing gave me confidence to see this through to the end. I'm humbled by your tireless efforts.

Lastly, to a multitude of clients, colleagues, friends and family members who have shared their wisdom, taught me lessons about life and business, and shaped my character all along the way. You lent me your ear, gave me valuable feedback, and stuck with me through thick and thin. I owe you a debt of gratitude I can never pay back. Instead, you have my promise that I'll pay it forward every day in every way that I possibly can.

About The Author

Steve Monte is a business and career coach who loves helping others accomplish their most serious goals. He also works as manager for the mental health clinic at Santa Clara County Juvenile Hall, helping youth get their lives back on track. Steve is an accomplished public speaker, mental healthcare consultant, writer, and CEO of Steve Monte Coaching. He helps aspiring young professionals become the managers, leaders, and executives of tomorrow's workforce while achieving the kind of work-life balance that eludes the masses.

Those who work with Steve learn to define success on their own terms, discover their life's purpose, and get things done for their companies, themselves, and their communities. With more than 10 years of experience in the counseling industry, Steve brings a wealth of practical knowledge to his coaching work, including the ability to listen intently and give feedback that's right on target.

Steve received his Master's degree in Social Work from Indiana University, with a focus on non-profit management and organizational leadership. He is also a licensed clinical social worker, and is registered with the California Board of Behavioral Sciences. Steve lives in Santa Clara, California with his wife Bethany and their son Noah. When he's not working, Steve likes to climb mountains, watch sunsets, and listen to waves crash on white, sandy beaches (preferably in foreign countries).